35865

Arts Media Group was formed in 1984 to establish a media campaign for community, Black and minority arts groups. It aims to provide a focussed response to media misrepresentation as it affects Black and minority arts and initiate debate. It offers advice and information to groups and organisations and courses on arts administration and media skills. Arts Media Group co-publishes with Minorities Arts Advisory Service, Black Arts in London magazine.

D1512693

Published in 1988 by ARTS MEDIA GROUP
90 DE BEAUVOIR RD LONDON N1 4EN Tel 254 6256/249 0994
©ARTS MEDIA GROUP, KWESI OWUSU, JACOB ROSS,
DAVID A. BAILEY and IAN WATTS.
DESIGNED BY SUE DRANSFIELD.
FRONT COVER PHOTOGRAPH BY JACOB ROSS.

BRITISH LIBRARY CATALOGUING IN PUBLICATION

Owusu, Kwesi
Behind the masquerade: the story of Notting Hill Carnival. 1.
London. (London Borough) Kensington and Chelsea.
Notting Hill. Street carnivals, to 1987
I. Title II. Ross, Jacob
394.2'5'0942134

ISBN 0-9512770-0-6

Distributed by Central Books, 14 The
Leathermarket, London SE1 3ER.

SWANSEA COLLEGE LIBRARY
TY COCH ROAD, SWANSEA
WEST GLAMORGAN. SA2 9EB

TO JOHN MILLINGTON, A VETERAN OF NOTTING HILL CARNIVAL, WHO LEFT US SO SUDDENLY. WALK HOME IN TRIUMPH

supported by City Limits

**CITY
LIMITS**
MAGAZINE
LONDON'S GUIDE

Arts Media Group acknowledges financial assistance from the Arts Council of Great Britain and Greater London Arts.

CONTENTS

ACCESSION No. 35865

SWANSEA COLLEGE LIBRARY
700.103 ow6
CLASS No. 394.250 wu

INTRODUCTION

Carnival is a passionate and celebratory landscape of Black working class experience. It reverberates with simmering voices, visions and deep resonances of historical memory. Every year it pays homage to a complex interplay of political and creative forces. It is also a rehearsal ground for future dramas and mass rituals of social reckoning.

In Britain today, Carnival is a symbol of Black aspirations and a reliable barometer of what a go on in our community. As an alternative aesthetic synthesis to the plastic statis of much of contemporary culture, it affirms the beauty and sheer vitality of the natural creative impulse and initiative. These are increasingly being suppressed by the dominance of electronic media and distorted by market forces.

The significance of carnival's aesthetic synthesis and its impact on contemporary culture are yet to be fully acknowledged. Present appreciation vacillate between poles of stereotypes; the overtly racist, which merely sees Carnival as an exotic event of jollification, and the attempts by race relations agencies and the Police to use the occasion for empty multi-racial gesturing. Not surprisingly, many London dailies do not miss the opportunity to grace front pages with pictures of policemen kissing Black women and babies. In addition to these stereotypes, numerous racist 'commonsense' understandings deduced from dominant ideologies operate. Particularly strong is the idea which associates the origins of carnival with Christianity and European Colonisers in the Americas.

In this book, we deal with this subtle negation of Black initiative by exploring the overwhelming Africaness of Carnival. A fascinating aspect of Carnival in both the Caribbean and Britain is the extent to which it has retained its African character and spirit in spite of the momentous dislocations of African people through the Atlantic slave trade and the apparent fragmentation of cultural identities by colonialism and contemporary nationhood. This is a conceptual problem which is often compounded by the difficulty of finding the appropriate language to talk about Carnival. All too often we tend to use very formalist or structuralist language to describe a highly creative experience which defies neat compartmentalisation and conventional ways of seeing. It is in fact a paradox, highlighted by the failure of the 'observer' to experience a cultural process which is simultaneously emotional and creative. "You see, carnival is not fun alone; is not just a time for colour clash and rainbow-play when even God sheself has to take a back seat an watch we people cascading out into the day to fill the skybowl with chants an songs an sounds an movement..., ... more than anything else, it is the celebration of emergence..., ... the destruction of the imposed semantic mould..." Here we explore a discourse that allows emotions and intellect to collide freely on an aesthetic field of political and cultural meaning and significance.

In spite of its present status as the biggest mass street event in Europe, it still suffers chronic underfunding and exploitation by an array of commercial interests such as the breweries, advertising agencies, London Transport, British Airways and British Tourist Board. This undermines efforts towards self-sufficiency and increases dependency on the State. Not surprisingly it is perhaps the most expressive and culturally volatile terrain on which the battle of positions between the Black Community and the State are ritualised.

As an expression of Black culture it is simultaneously contemporary and historical. Its contemporariety is assumed on the streets as the revellers and mass players recreate their lives and hopes in the shadows of socio-political issues and agendas. The people play mass ritualising Black experience as it engages the matrix of state institutions and socio-political forces. But Carnival is also deeply historical and symbolic. The interaction of historical and contemporary elements give to Carnival its dynamism and relevance as a powerful force that has the potential of great creative transformation. □

Kwesi Owusu and Jacob Ross

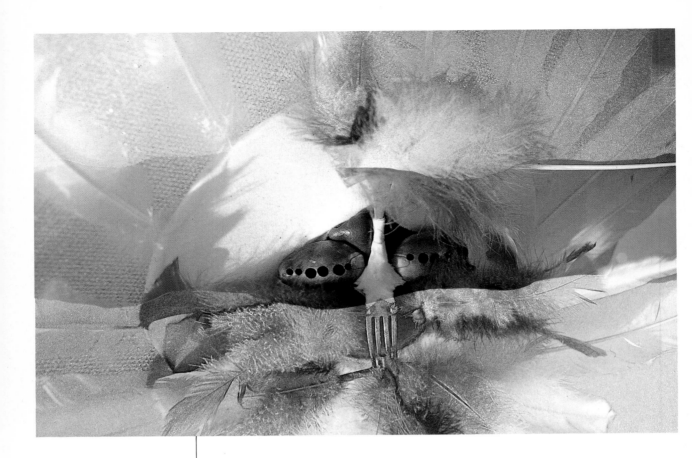

MASQUERADE

On the road with the masquerade you don't see what you normally see. Voices hurry the boats to sea, shadows dance in the wind, blue-eyed dragons and sasabonsam inhale fire and belch out smoke. On the road with the masquerade you don't feel what you normally feel. Little chimes, arrow and *shack-shack* take a walk with Ananse and brigades of dancing feet along the valleys of the Kilimanjaro. There, sunrise is as sure as the volcano surge from the belly of the earth. On the road with the masquerade you don't do what you normally do. Voices wrap around the bass line and wings flap free like birds in the blue caribbean sky. On the road with the masquerade chains dangle loose in the dusty clouds when the people surge forward. Sound systems stay on freedom grooves and the long play of history spins and spins round the African Sun.

On the road with the masquerade, you don't use words you normally use. Soon come says the hurricane in the murmmurings of the gentle breeze. Grandma feels the power in the message for it speaks at the junction of bolts and thunder. When it's ready it rushes home like Nanny on the threshold of reckoning. On the road with the masquerade, you don't hear what you normally hear. Languages long scattered by the winds of the Atlantic Crossing surge forth in unison and children whisper to each other; its chantwell time now, its chantwell time now and the power Black' and the echo takes it away. 'Splendid ebony cast, worker-wise and history-deep'. The masquerade stands poised on the edge of the storm. A million eyes feed the hands and colours splash on the imagination of the story tellers of our time.

The moment of the masquerade is a beauty that answers the call of a deep yearn and dream. Nature nods. There is the colour green and fresh leaf smiling. There is gold, metal-rich and precious. there is red, sap-deep and simmering on a landscape saluting the sun. Violet dazzles from the rear of a Star Trek and purple tails a full moon glow. The heart is kneaded in song and it softens the metallic drench of tear drops. Behind the masquerade the people get ready for tomorrow. □

It's a day to Carnival and All Saints road is draped in full colour. A fervent dress rehearsal of popular creativity is moving into top gear and everyone is busy. Old and young Rastafari mount sound systems and the boxes pile up, occasionally meeting first-floor windows. The wires connect all possible power points along the street. They go into equalisers and amplifiers like masses of centipedes. All the small cafes are opened, even the ones which get little business during the year are jammed. The air is charged with expectation and anxiety. 'Testing . . . Testing . . .' says the Dee Jay. A police patrol car speeds past. 'Just testing . . .' A few systems are ready to go and one or two are already on medium decibels. Freddie MacGregor sings 'Somewhere' in a soulful mellow voice and a man freezes into a pose as warm textured sounds peel off the speakers. Trappe John is on the DM7 and he makes the synthesiser wail in calculated charges, heartfelt and deep.

The floats are packed in front of Mangrove Restaurant. Some pans are already mounted and a drum kit is being crowned with cymbals. A bass man is striking chords of irreverent melodies. The floats are sprayed with red paint. Today the colour grey does not show and cellotape covers all hints of urban rust. The men chat, smoking and drinking rum and whisky. The floats are nearly ready and by the morn they shall rise from the sea bed of saints and trail the streets and sidewalks of joy, dancing to the rhythms of the urban Black experience. □

Upstairs at the Mangrove, the mas camp is in full swing. The people are busy putting finishing touches to the costumes and masks. The big day is only hours away and each passing minute is precious. A magazine pull-out of a carnival gone hangs from the wall, almost falling. Months of work have been squeezed into days and the strain might have proved overwhelming if not for the high moments of inspired creativity transforming wire, cane, paint, leather, paste, card and cloth into objects of beauty.

D.A. BAILEY

Spirits are high and the people create earnestly. Their faces glow with pleasurable anticipation; of tomorrow's masquerades, the teeming crowds, the metallic drench of steel pan rhythms and carefree children kicking empty beer cans along the streets. There are also moments of silence and apprehension, the kind to seperate a thought and movements of the hand but they only invite insistent voices criss crossing warmly.

For many here carnival time is meeting old friends, making new ones and finding out what a big boy auntie's son is now. They rarely have time to chat or even meet sometimes, except perhaps the flying visit or the occasional 'how you do' on Portobello market or at the street corner. Smiles casually punctuate conversation and story lines coax old memories. More smiles. It is a refreshing break from the factory floor, the supermarket till and the typing booth. 'Nice one', a woman's voice slips into the fray of admiration as another tries on a costume. A foot moves tentatively into a leather sandal. The sole is too small. □

She may be a seamstress, a garment factory worker or just one of the many African mothers who has learnt to sew and mend garments. Few African households can do without mother's sewing tin packed to the brim with pairs of scissors, needles, balls of wool and thread. There is the kid's shirt to patch, there is baby's new cardigan to knit and new patterns in British Home Stores' catalogue to try. When she was

D.A. BAILEY

leaving the Caribbean grandma gave her an old sewing machine. It was a manual, a Singer model and to be honest with you, it has seen better days. When she first tried to use it, she had to pour a whole tin of oil into it to activate the motor. Grandma insisted she came with it, 'never know when you need it' she said. Today it reminds her of the long evenings in the open yard sewing and patching flour sacks and pillow cases, and when grandma was in a good mood, a dress for herself.

Grandma has a small stall in the market and she always goes with the sewing machine. When business isn't so good she would send her to her friends and all who knew her, to patch a few clothes for a few shillings. She would balance the portable machine gracefully on her head and click the pairs of scissors to an insistent rhythm in her head. In West Africa we call people who earn money visiting and mending clothes 'Oye adie yie' (Person who mends and makes things better). They usually have a hook line of a popular song on their lips and children are always at hand to respond with a chorus or a song of their own.

> I am a little child
> With no money
> My clothes are torn
> 'Oye adie yie' please mend them and make things better.

Grandma used to say sewing a dress was like going through life. You have to go diligently; not too fast to miss out the colourful embroidery or too slow to miss the outing. There are the trying moments and possible disasters. Some needles are quite difficult to thread and a stubborn garment can break it. It could be your last needle. A careless swerve of the scissors can also ruin a beautiful dress. Grandma is diligent in life. Her skill and intelligence inform her creativity and attitudes to life.

The consciousness is ancient. She herself may have been initiated into it by foreparents and the ancestral knowledge stretches backwards like a simmering silver line in the family memory. The Atlantic crossing was momentous, not least in the suppression of aspects of African culture which proved 'subversive' to the slave system. Drumming by African slaves was for example, periodically banned because slaves on different estates used it to communicate. African languages were also discouraged. The slave and colonial experience has resulted in severe mutations in our contemporary consciousness. It means that we have to negotiate the expression of the silver line at every turn and within each space of our modern cultures. But you see, we are a people of messages, signals, the hyroglyphics and allusive speech and it is impossible to legislate or hammer out of existence what is seond nature and lurking at the threshold of reckoning.

Her foreparents may have come from Bonwire in precolonial Africa. There in Asante, the Community developed one of the most successful weaving cultures in the world. Kente and Adinkra are its more well known products. Proverb patterns and socio-political imagery are woven together with colourful thread. When the cloth is worn it functions as a lingual tapestry depicting social mood, political association and ideological schism.

In the 1960's President Kwame Nkrumah presented a gift from the people of Bonwire to the United Nations; a giant size kente symbolising world peace.

Grandma connects the tradition of Bonwire through the silver line and the instinctive/intuitive centres of remembrance. Carnival creativity is an act of historical reclamation, a departure from the alienating routine of Capitalist labour. It connects the creative energy to the African experience. ☐

This year (1986) Mangrove is playing **'Me Myself I warrior!** *'All oppressed people of the world are warriors. We must be — to survive.'* explains Arthur Peters, the designer who co-ordinates the creative process at the camp. A quiet unassuming man, he moves around the room, discreetly, purposely, offering ideas and skills and hinting at creative possibilities. He is a formidable inspiration at Mangrove and an innovator in the Carnival tradition both in Notting Hill and Port of Spain, Trinidad. Over the years he has contributed to the creation of mas memorable for their ingenuity and beauty.

L WATS

I. WATTS

A Visit to Disneyland (1974) was a mark of his hand. It was a fascinating adventure in mas making, a magical journey to Disneyland which transformed familiar Disney characters with imaginative sculpture work and customery. The following year he was in Trinidad Carnival with **'To Hell with you,'** designed with Peter Minshall, then his apprentice. **'Paradise Lost'** made interesting use of his wire-bending techniques.

Wire bending is crucial to the construction of Carnival sculptures. It stabilises the infrastructure; the bare skeleton which is then elaborated and splashed with colour and ornaments. Carnival sculptures, should in spite of size, be strong enough to last days of gruelling duty, and at the same time, have the flexibility to facilitate easy and subtle movements. This is the test for each mas camp. On the road the sculpture should be able to dance when it is brought to life by masqueraders who stretch its durability to the limits. □

J. ROSS

Clothes say so much about ourselves. They hint at our moods and anxieties, the little things that make us happy and sad, our dreams and fears and much more. Each morning and sundown we drape our bodies with personal inuendo and social meaning, expressing ourselves on the conscious and sub-conscious. Some of us wear clothes as flags of intention and pleasure, social power and status. Sometimes we wear them for convenience and occasion, at all times, to articulate a complex range of ideological and emotional variables.

Clothes are sign posts of cultural identity and desire. They reflect the moods of times and temperaments of generations. As Africans in the West our choices and our options filter through a regulatory valve of dominant European values informed by environmental factors. The specific cultural meanings and nuance of tradition which we bring to our personalities are at the best of times lurking behind European aesthetics.

Africa gave to Europe, the art of weaving through the Egyptian civilization. But when the modern era dawned with the European voyages, it is said that Columbus kissed the brow of the Guinea Coast in an Iberian cassock. Since then Africans have worn European clothes. We wear them to work, to school, to church, to the penitentiary and to bed. We dream in them. At Carnival time the process is inverted for you connect the silver line and make your own clothes. You make it special, load it with a baggage of your own treasures and make it speak your language. You make what you want and you call it your own. □

I. WATTS

T. FIOR

J. ROSS

'Destroying Angels' was created with cocoyea mas in 1983. Masqueraders in hell-size wings turned a West London Street into a celestial zone jammed with brisk brigades of dancing feet entrapped by Soca and voices. When night fell they appeared, in their glitter, to be filtering through a mosaic of stars and spitfire. **'When the Spirit moves'** (1985) was Mangrove's prelude to **'Me Myself I Warrior'**, a theme inspired by Burkinabe culture in West Africa. The interpreted designs from Burkina Faso are lavishly embellished with colour; prime colours which rubricate the thin delicate lines of ink. Asymetrical patterns of black and red also merge with semi-circular shapes of white tempered with yellow stripes.

In Bunkina Faso the colours evoke the tropical environment. The art is an allusion to the beauty of the natural landscape — deep brown is for the soil, jaded yellow for fallen leaves blowing in the harmattan breeze and lustrous pink for sundown. The people pay homage to the rivers, the fresh water ponds and grasslands. Invariably costumes are made of leather, wood and finished off with tall blades of grass. The inter-action with nature is the source of life and culture. The costumes function as work clothes for hunters, the camouflage which helps them to blend with the landscape as they pursue game.

Hunters have intimate knowledge of the natural world. As they hunt, they reproduce sounds to synchronised movements evoking a multi-process fusion of work and creativity. This fusion is also symbolised by the simultaneous act of a farmer's cutlass swing and work dance. Mangrove made a link with this tradition and interpreted its significance to the Black urban reality in Britain.

One of the things which struck me (KO) on a recent visit to Burkina Faso was the accuracy of **'When the Spirit Moves'** to the local tradition. The designs were remarkably identical and the colours appeared as mere elements of a tapestry created by the same people. It was a hot afternoon in front of Maison Des Peuple in Ouagadougou, a dry, sprawling city sitting on the edge of the Sahara. As the masquerades from Koko, Warba and Tibin hit dust into the sky I wondered how the two traditions kept in touch in spite of the physical distance between them and the apparent seperateness of national identities. Notting Hill is a few thousand miles away from Ouagadougou. It is also locked up in the concrete jungle of Babylon. Here the official language is French. Colonialism bequeaths some striking buildings of Parisien architecture which stand in the shadows of Mossi designed Mosques. Every so often, during the day, a steady voice rings out from the domes calling the city to prayer. Every face turns to Mecca and foreheads humbly touch the sand. Ouagadougou is also the capital of a very poor country, with one of the lowest gross national product in the world if a United Nations Statistic of the late 70's is still valid.

From the apparent labyrinth of dissimilarity emerges continuity; a life

line which evokes the essence of the African experience by defying the geo-political boundaries of our modern culture. The mas people of Notting Hill are warriors in the concrete complex of Babylon. They engage it in their daily lives, defying the rugged contours of its plastic landscape. In Ouagadougou, Mangrove's creative power is energised when the dust goes up with hand and feet thrashing the breeze and sky.

The sound builds up into a thunderous roar and the horns bellow with the force of the winds. A masquerader moves to the centre of the circle and somersaults on two sticks. His huge frame spins in the air and folds like cloth around the intoxicated patterns of sound. The intensity of the occasion is like the climax of a Carnival street jam and if you listen carefully, you will feel soca, osode, rumba, and one drop-rhythm in the music from Koko and Warba. □

K. OWUSU

T. FIORI

Come closer so I can hear you beyond the oceans, the border check-points and the small visa print in your passport. Come closer so I can whisper to you like the water that drips from your roof in Trenchtown. Come closer so you can hear me from Bronx, Handsworth and the little village not on the map. Come closer so I can see my face in yours and yours in mine. Come closer my sister, brother and mother for you wouldn't feel the thud of my heart beat on Capital Radio or the full range of my tonal chords on your compact disc. Come closer my uncle from Djibouti and Auntie who emigrated to Canada. This hand here and the finger there touch the notes on Coltrane's horn and sister Holiday's voice woke grandpa after a sad, sad night. My hands hold a little guord vibrating with a song you used to sing. Come closer, take a step, up the escalator, a tube ride on the freedom train towards home. □

All over Notting Hill preparations for Carnival are underway. People carry on their business scrupulously, barely lifting their eyes to meet others and say 'how you do'. Some shuffle boxes, cooking utensils and equipment on the pavements, whilst others wire up speakers, turntables and amplifiers. The kids are excited to see so many people outside and they run after each other kicking down arranged boxes in the process. Parents yell at them ceaselessly. They could do better; like help them to set up the food stalls and the little improvised street cafes. A lone man passes by dancing to a beat in his head. Some of the men wish him well. The children wouldn't let him be. They walk up All Saints road, behind him doing robotic versions of his carefully contrived movements. A bunch of balloons jerks out of the hands of a baby and makes for the skyline. A yell of disappointment follows the colourful climb up the grey roofs.

On Westbourne Park road the banners and flags are already up and drink sellers have made little mole hills out of beer cans and Pepsi. Enticing aroma of rice and curry goat fill the air as hot plates pass hands. Here the celebrations have obviously started for some revellers. Their feet move to electro funk and the rapid sound fire of New York rappers. Their voices grow louder as we approach Portobello road. They conspire to be heard above the music from the record shops and the small mono spinners playing old, ska, mento and Lord Bill Barnes.

Lord Bill sings in a smooth and sublime tone, conjuring the idyllic image of the Caribbean as a tropical tourist paradise — sunny, palm lined

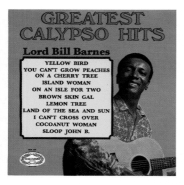

GREATEST CALYPSO HITS

Lord Bill Barnes

YELLOW BIRD
YOU CAN'T GROW PEACHES
ON A CHERRY TREE
ISLAND WOMAN
ON AN ISLE FOR TWO
BROWN SKIN GAL
LEMON TREE
LAND OF THE SEA AND SUN
I CAN'T CROSS OVER
COCOANUT WOMAN
SLOOP JOHN B.

beaches, rum and amorous people. His voice soars nostalgically accompanied by acoustic guitar, hand drums and flute. The older folk miss the tenderness in such a voice in today's hard edge music. A couple is sat by the small speaker tapping their feet and all ears. Lord Bill sings 'You can't grow peaches on a Cherry Tree' and they know it very well. Its a love song and its probably the way he sings it that makes it so relevant to them.

I have tried to make you love me
I have done everything your way
And I am crying for the words you never said,
You think love is an illusion
That must end inside a conclusion
If that's what you feel
Then that's just what it would be
And you can't grow peaches on a cherry tree

When I see peaches blossom
I'll regret I said goodbye
I'll remember cherry kisses and I'll cry
but I can't go on pretending

J. ROSS

That our love is never ending
For you can't be loved
Unless you want to be
And you can't grow peaches on a cherry tree
Someday I'll find a new love
But for you that can't be no love
For you can't be loved
Unless you want to be

Lord Bill's voice stirs memories and tails off into Soca as we move on. On Portobello road the crowd is growing and the chic parlours of jewelry and clothes are full. Here the antique dealer meets the local street vendor and there are of course the street posers from the posh outlays of Holland Park. They shuffle their feet to Reggae but it could be Spandau Ballet, Wham or Curiosity Killed the Cat, for all we know. Their ears are cocked with Walkman earphones and their movements just do not synchronise with the music.

I. WATTS

I. WATTS

From the drab buildings above some old folk stare at the cheerful people below occasionally waving to familiar faces.

Under the westway flyover sound engineers wire up a huge PA system and prepare Carnival's prime music spot. It is a focus for revellers. They come from all directions and gather under the huge canopy, ringed by food sellers and many others selling a broad range of merchandise. Many up and coming and established bands have played here. The cheers normally go up with a thousand whistles and the excitement here is considerable. It is passed on like electric. Today the space is almost bare except a few people putting up stalls and other bits of infrastructure. A loud shriek vibrates from the PA. People cock their ears, their faces contoured with displeasure.

A small alleyway seperates the music canopy from the office of the Carnival Arts Committee. There is a queue to use the intercom at the door and we are told its really hectic up there. The small office with a skeleton staff co-ordinates a celebration of a million revellers. On the last day the office is literally beseiged by anyone who has any business to do with Carnival. There are the stall holders, mas people and bands seeking last minute information on places and routes, the sound systems whose allocated sites are too small for their equipment, there are the stewards bringing back information on this arrangement and that operation, the Police, Ambulance service, fire brigade, pursuing their own priorities and of course the journalists and public seeking information on events and happenings.

The office delegates organisational responsibility to members of the Carnival Committee. They are all busy in their own homes and small offices, concluding logistics and details of events. □

LAST YEARS KING OF KINGS WINNERS

☆ **GENESIS** ☆

INVITE YOU TO THE

LAUNCHING
OF THEIR 1986 LONDON CARNIVAL
COSTUME BAND

SAT 5th JULY 1986
9pm till LATE

AT 315 Kensal Road, (off Ladbroke Grove)
London W10

★COSTUME DESIGNS ON DISPLAY★
MUSIC BY
LORD SAM   SOCA.WAX

BAR & FOOD
Admission £1.50   Phone: 903 6346

This is Kensal Road on the other side of Ladbroke Grove. It runs almost parallel to the little canal that flows along the tower blocks overlooking Harmon road and Meanwhile Gardens. On Carnival day, revellers from Kensal Rise, Harlsden and beyond take to it, eager to find a short route to the nerve centres of celebration. It is predominantly residential but resembling a busy industrial street of yesterday. If it was, the life has been sucked out of it. On this Summer's day a few fitters from a nearby garage are out on the streets, fidgeting with this or that car spare part and enjoying the sun.

The signboard for Genesis Mas Camp looks prominent. On this grey street it appears to curve an imposing presence for itself. There is a constant stream of people entering the house and a buzz of conversation on the ground floor. When people leave, the goodbyes are long enough to be completed with a shout from the pavements, and occasionally with a hoot of a car's horn. One of the well-established and fascinating mas of Notting Hill's getting ready for tomorrow. In 1985 Genesis Mas won the **'King of Kings'** award and it is leaving no stone unturned to make another impression.

The theme for tomorrow is **'Ancient Japanese'** and there is activity on all floors of the house. Spare rooms are full with finished and half-finished Costumes and Sculptures. In what was originally the front room of the house, members of the band and visitors sit on the edge of every inch of space engrossed in communal conversation. The kitchen is next to the front room. It is also crowded with people cooking and selling soft drinks. On the top floor is the main costume-making space. The colour for tomorrow is obviously red and the mas people have cut them into a hundred shapes and sizes and are now applying shiny beads and metal as embroidery. The interpretations of **'Ancient Japanese'** partly hinge on royal pageantry and the ceremonial. Little triangles centred with mirrors hunging from the walls are waiting to be elaborated. Vernon Williams, the co-ordinator of the camp is out to get a few materials and he is expected back soon. □

D.A. BAILEY

D.A. BAILEY

D.A. BAILEY

No limers, time wasters or bad-vibe spirits. It's strictly workers when you cross this threshold here. Unlike the conveyor belt, the time-clocks and voices of supervisors which make your stomach churn, we are our own bosses here. We decide on what we produce, laughing elephants, sandals for the kids or a city of the new women, men and children we all want to be. We choose our own materials — bright-coloured cloth and ribbon, silk and sparkling beads or the old garment grandma gave to brother Louie. We work our own hours, eat, drink and laugh when we want to. No deadline has beaten us yet. Thousands will be there, rain or shine, giving form and movement to what we create. They jump in them and smile to the skies because they didn't pick them up from the supermarket. There is history in these hands and I worker has created since time begun. □

My dear one, moments of peaceful solitude are scattered in the labyrinth of our daily lives. We warriors have to find them to keep them. My dear little one, it is difficult to achieve even the little things we dream about; so always listen carefully. Feel the moments of silence so that you can see danger when it approaches. Remember the gas meter only takes what comes from the royal mint. The city worships the sound of the coin and has a padded stone for a heart. We walk with our songs simmering within. So whenever we sing it overwhelms the city and the traffic lights jam on red. My dear one, you are a warrior and that is what your uncle from Bamako always wished. You speak his mind and dance to his spirit when you trail the contours of this concrete landscape. Son, today is our day. □

I. WATTS

I. WATTS

I. WATTS

D.A.BAILEY

I. WATTS

I. WATTS

J ROSS

HISTORY

Can't beat we drum
In My own, my native land
Can't have we Carnival
In my own, my native land
In my own, my native land . . .

The sharp lament rises above the barrack yards and hangs threatening, like a knife-arm, potent with the protest-venom. The police have retreated, their courage drowned by voices that roll and crash like breakers on the town.

Can't have we Bacchanal
In my own, my native land . . .

The cane plantations — bitter more than sweet — spill their guts out in smoke-choked rage, smoulders: conflagate. And the angry-river, fire-bitter flood of words continue to mix and merge, shuddering the tall walls of respectability.

In my own, my native land
In my own, my native land

The year is 1881 — the Canboulay riots — when a 'major armed clash between the Trinidad colonial police and the 'local' population occurred,' following a decision to clamp down on the Carnival celebrations of that year.

The barrack-yards of Port of Spain, where the 'Diametres' ruled, presided over neighbourhoods, nurtured loyalties, honed and hoarded the weapons of survival for confrontations such as these, gathered their bands of revellers turned warriors and went forth to defy and try the governor.

The batallions converged, conferred — women-warriors and child-soldiers, chorused the call of 'chantwells' whose razor-tongues had been shaped and sharpened by the unending rehearsal days and nights in the yard-bands of the town. The collective mind conspired and condemned: and suddenly, like God, Herself, they created. Hands reached for sticks; made bones of them. Grass was made flesh. Stones became eyes; discarded garments, the apparel to bedeck a king. Moments, and an effigy of the governor stood in the centre of the square. It was stoned, then tried, then charged; then burnt!

Carnival is fun!
Come, let us talk . . .

Not so much about the *origins* of Carnival but more importantly, perhaps, about the *spirit* of the thing. Regarding origins, the facts and arguments are not totally resolved. From the historians who have started and stuck with the Trinidad Carnival, we learn that Carnival

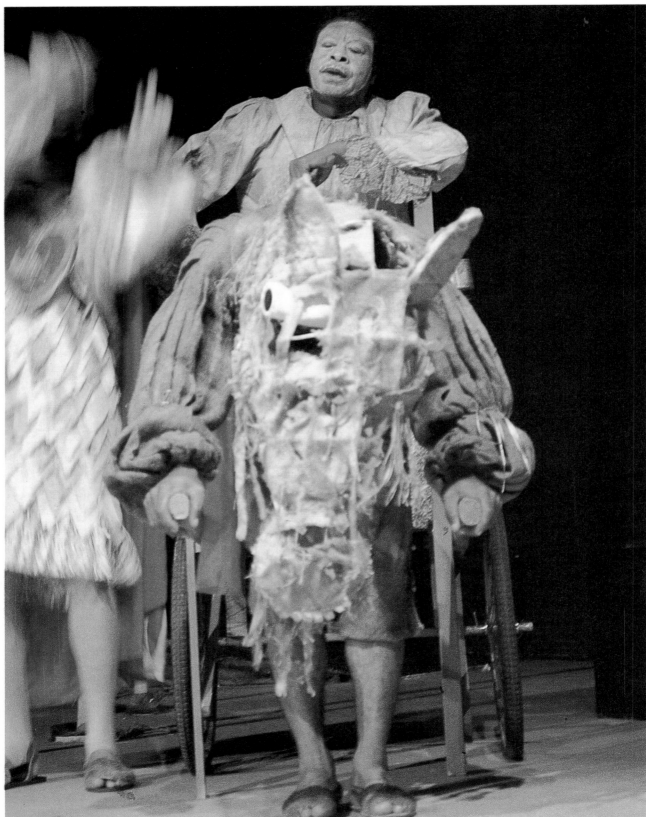

J. ROSS

constituted a high point of the élite French Creole social season, running from Christmas to Ash Wednesday. 'A time of 'brilliant divertissement' and contagious gaiety, brilliant verbal sallies and comic bufoonery which made the subject of the next day's conversation.'

Allegedly, the Africans in the Caribbean copied the format and added their essence — a theory that presents more questions than answers particularly in the light of other 'celebrations' elsewhere, as in Brazil, Cuba, Barbados with its 'Crop Over' equivalent, and no French Creole influence to boot.

Now, as early as 1847 Carnival in the islands had already developed 'the prototypes of the mass, open-air extravaganzas of the Carnival we know today': the mass processions, the uniformed, rainbow-coloured pageantry, the pride, pleasure and *consumate expertise* in mocking the hell out of king, queen, governor, priest and all the representatives of ruling class authority. The following 'observations' could have come from any contemporary, fundamentally foreign commentator on any one of the Carnivals across the two continents: *Two grand processions one . . . a canopy of red, glazed calico, trimmed with silver tinsel, shading a royal pair who in conscious majesty sat within representing the sovereign pair of England. This brilliant cortege(is) marshalled forwards by a huge NEGRO who stalked along, spear in hand, as if intent on dire needs.* Dire deeds, indeed!

You see, Carnival is not fun alone; is not just a time of colour-clash and rainbow-play when even God Sheself has to tek a back seat an watch *we* people cascading out into the day to fill the sky-bowl wit chants an songs an sounds an movement: is not just a time to send up commanding hands, gather stars and moons to earth and sew them on to captive garments that flutter-fly and wind-flow in rivers of silver glimmerings.

More than anything else, it is the celebration of emergence, an affirmation of survival and *continuity*; the destruction of the imposed semantic mould. The calling of the world to question. The wise ones become fools; the preacher, devil. Pregnant men parade their pain. White is blackened; and black is blackened deeper black. Women rise on stilts above the earth, stand twenty feet tall, looking down upon the doll-house homes whose daily oppressions have hardened the hands and steeled the hearts. Carnival is the culmination of more than three centuries of struggle against a system designed, as Walter Rodney puts it, 'to kill'.

The Caiso, 'In My Own, My Native Land,' represents one of the first recorded expressions of positive nationalism in the Eastern Caribbean. The symbolic burning of the governor has a deeper basis than the mere spontaneous bout of indignation to an oppressive piece of legislation. It echoes faithfully a fundamental theme that underlies Afro-Caribbean culture throughout; that is the relentless deployment of an arsenal of strategies — cultural and otherwise — to survive.

The Africans who arrived brought with them languages, religion and a complex matrix of relationships with each other and Earth Mother. Dispossessed, uprooted, bewildered; yes: but Africa was there — in the blood.' From day one, the resistance began to the cultural and physical means employed by the Europeans to sever all sense of roots. The old knowledge buried in the bones seeped through the flesh, and guided fingers to hollow trees, make drums — each note that rode the angry winds, punishable by death or mutilation. The songs of Dahomey, Yoruba, Mandingo, Ibo, Kormanti... silenced. The gods retreated.

The Twi, Fanti, Wolof, tongues were sliced. Africa back-tracked, assessed the enemy, re-emerged. Now Shango sang the hymns of Christian gods with the rhythm and dance of Africa, preserving meaning. The Niger-Congo structured the words of Europe, reshaped sounds and meanings in its own image and likeness. Ananse abdicated god-hood, became the 'weak' and clever spider that tutored generations born there, the subtitles of warfare. Carnival is the single phenomenon that brings all of these forces together. The divide has often been very thin indeed between the un-inhibited jump of jollification and the firm-footed march of reckoning. Beneath the fixed smile of the mask the coiled frown lurks. If Canboulay was a fight between bands where individual 'stickmen' resolved their inter-personal rivalries and waged regional warfare against other bands, in 1881, 'it took on the character of a historical underclass in united action against the police.' In 1882, Trinidad again — riot this time in San Fernando when the state tried to limit 'Playing' till 9.00 p.m.

1973, Grenada: devil mas (jab-jab) was banned because respectable citizens complained that their pretty white clothes were stained with black paint. The following year, the highest number of Devil Mas ever recorded hit the street of St. George's. Months later, for different but connected reasons a 'Canboulay' style trial of the nation's leader by ten thousand people resulted in a verdict of twenty-five crimes against the people.

In 1980 masqueraders packed the streets of Toronto. Steel drums, strung on stands gushed cataracts of polyphonous rhythms. In North America, Africa met and celebrated another successful implantation — another root dug deep. Above the shift and throb and buzz, radio stations prattled inane commentaries, applying alien logic to the spectacle of grey asphalt streets transformed, blossoming a galaxy of stars and suns. The narrow mould of reasoning strained to contain the vast and moving ocean that controlled the streets of Babylon. Radios rattled, grated. Wonder-struck 'natives' gaped and ear-clung to the tiny reassurance of their tiny transistorised radio-voices. Toronto thundered. Somewhere on one of the many channels covering the celebrations, a tiny voice rattled. The commentator signalled a 'return

J. ROSS

J. ROSS

to studio'. A commercial assailed the ear, advertising German lager. Background voices. Someone had forgotten 'to close' the announcer's microphone. A voice asked a voice if he was going down to see the Carnival. A voice answered that he didn't think so; 'don't see any sense in going down there just to watch those niggers jumping around on our streets.' The radio crackled. Someone exclaimed. Sudden realisation. The microphone was closed in panic. The commercial ended quickly followed by another, advertising a Japanese car. Too late. Listeners had heard. Those at home readying themselves to join the celebrations later in the day immediately left their flats, the rented rooms and houses. They joined the throng, passing the indignation on to a brother, a sister, cousin, nephew, nen-nen, friend. The music no longer flowed. The dancing slowed; became a march of purpose towards the radio station. Police arrived to curb the confrontation.

The history of the growth of Carnival reflects also the deepening of ruling class unease and their consequent efforts to either curb or control it. In the Caribbean, legislation and efforts to enforce them were supported by the church, in particular. The Lenten season follows the Carnival. A time of holy penitence and contrition by the masses for the 'excesses' of the past days of revelry. The guilt is pounded in by the

J. ROSS

J. ROSS

chiding cant of parish priests and wayside preachers. The school reminds the young that Carnival stems from the word, 'Carne': that which is of the flesh. The equation is extended: Carnival equals Bacchannal and Bacchannal stems from the word, Bacchus — the pagan god of wine and sin and wanton song. That which is of the devil.

The masquerade is over. The calypso *season* ended. Any rhythm that echoes Africa is deemed a gross profanity. Children, still bubbling with the remnants of the past days of drum-dance and colour-flow are chastised for chants that flowed freely from their lips just hours before. Even the calypsonians come to rest, acknowledging the period of ceasefire. Nevertheless, new song-seeds are being sown, inside their heads, soul-consoled that church and state and individual weilders of the oppressive rod are still bitter with the aftertaste of verbal bombs dropped on them by masqueraders chanting their 'road-marches'. The house-tall women have come to earth; the stars and moons released: the rainbow given back its colours. The lion sleeps. □

The Calypso

The Calypso is both blood-relation and life-blood of the Carnival. It sets the mood, the tone and rhythm of every year's event. The equation is simple: no calypso, no carnival. More than any other form of cultural expression and *precisely* because of the perceived threat it poses to the status quo, it has had to fight off attacks by those it often threatens. Calypsonians have always fought — and within the past decade — have begun to win the struggle for recognition *outside* of the annual Carnival arena.

The extempore tradition of creating songs that challenged and mocked, social and political power and ensured collective participation was developed a long time before Carnival was developed as a politico-cultural institution. It is an important tributary that flows into the stream of Carnival but it has a seperate and continuing function in society that must not be ignored. Until recently, colonial and 'neo-' colonial systems in the Caribbean were careful to impose a kind of 'season' on calypso. Calypso was only acceptable in the two or three months leading up to the Carnival celebrations. It stopped with the 'Lenten Season' and had to wait another year to spring forth. Calypsonians never stopped composing their songs in the yard, village or rum-shop gatherings throughout the year. Despite the tacit ban, calypso had no season. It recognised only the discipline of the collective mind listening to it, approving or disapproving.

True to the *spirit* of this tradition, calypsonian, Valentino claims that Calypso is the only opposition. More a critic than a griot, Gordon Rohler, predicates: 'The calypso is a mirror of the struggle for an egalitarian society, closely connected in each decade with the quest for (wo)manhood and identity.' The evolution of Caribbean society, the shifts and changes in attitudes, the subtleties and nuances inherent in these changes are nowhere better recorded than in the calypsoes created in those periods. **'Can't sing in myland'** not only recorded the growing sense of ownership of the land and identification with a culture that the predominantly African population has given shape and meaning to, but it is also a questioning of the right of aliens to create laws that controlled their lives. With the restructuring of the Crown Colony system, in 1954, the stirrings for the establishment of a Federation, and the continuation of the introduction of Universal sufferage — started in Jamaica and Trinidad in 1944, Atilla the Hun was bitterly attacking the injustice of British Imperial policy through his calypsoes — an uncompromising advocate for the demands of an awakened population. *'The major issues no longer revolve around the aspirations of the middle class but are set by working class demands,'* one observer pointed out. Atilla the Hun was jailed on account of his song.

45   Governments have lost elections as a result of calypsoes that exposed their failings to the public. Trinidad President Karl Hudson Philips lost all credibility after being thoroughly mauled by the Mighty Chalkdust's calypso 'Ah Fraid Karl' in the early 1980's. Milton Cato's Government, in July 1981 banned reigning calypso Monarch *'Lord Have Mercy's* calypso THEY RIGHT which, in murderously ironic tones, was pressuring the Saint Vincent Government to demolish its anti-people laws:

Dey right to increase de police force
De right to give dunce men some big post
An when dey protek criminals guilty of murder
*   An when dy neglect Troumaca, make de Grenadines suffer*
An wreck agriculture
I would say
Dey right!

The year before, the Mighty Sparrow, respecting no boundaries was commenting on the international scene and the sudden, dramatic fall of dictators around the globe:

The rule of the tyrants declined
In the Year 1979
From Uganda to Nicaragua
It's bombs and bullets all the time
So they corrupt, so defiled
So it's coup after coup all the while
Human rights they violate
They thought they were too great

Gairy is a wanted man
Idi Amin is a wanted man
Shah of Iran fighting hard to survive
He too is wanted, dead or alive . . .

In 1982, The Mighty Sparrow turned on Trinidad:

Hospitals have no linen
Is brown paper dey using

You terrible school system
Is such a bloody problem

Publication transportation is an abomination

We can't get house so we squat
Livin wit cockroach an rat

Your cesspit flowing over
You could catch yellow fever

This, in a nutshell, is calypso full-fledged, the ones that are listened to.
The songs of the sycophants pass and are never heard again. True
opposition never dies. □

NOTTING HILL

The masquerade runs through the heart of the Black Community of Notting Hill. It connects dreams to the lives of those who came from the Caribbean after the second world war. They came to fill up the bottom end of the labour market — driving the buses, sweeping the streets, collecting rubbish and restoring buildings dazed and scattered by German bombs. Some of them were fresh from the war, having confronted fascism from the rugged trenches across Europe and from the air. After the fall of Hitler most were discharged in the Caribbean. They were soon to board the steamers plying the Atlantic and re-register in the service of the mother country; this time piling up the bricks and turning the wheels of British post-war reconstruction.

The Empire Windrush docked in Tilbury in 1948. Other boats anchored at Southampton, Liverpool, Bristol and Plymouth. The train journey to London was fascinating for its fresh evocation of the English countryside with its apparent peacefulness and well orderliness. There is no hint here of the socially traumatic migrations of peasants to the cities during the industrial revolution and the sometimes bloody enforcement of the land enclosure acts. These acts imposed absolute rights of private property on land and effectively dispossessed the peasantry.

The arrivants stared through the windows and smelt the fresh, rustic air. Some could recognise a few sign-posts lodged in their memories by the colonial film or Christmas card. There were the well-kept hedges seperating the farms, the Stone Cottages with creeping plants on their roofs and the little canals meandering across the cultivated plots. Many were puzzled not to see more people, at least groups of farm workers tending the plots as in the Caribbean. Occasionally a lone worker smoking a pipe would appear beside the old tractor. He would wave and a whole carriage would respond. For some it was the only image to salvage the creeping realisation that the English countryside was virtually deserted.

> The vast majority of us never saw the countryside
> again for years, as our lives were to be trapped
> in the inner-city areas. At Paddington Station
> hundreds of our own people would be waiting
> to meet friends and relatives. Nevertheless, many
> were disappointed at finding no one to greet them
> and had to make their own way to the only address
> they had. (Tevor Carter, Shattering Illusions, West Indians in British
> Politics. 1985)

These were days of disappointing revelations. The unsung voices of the colonies had come to find their places in the heritage of empire but there were few decent vacancies. The problem was not so much starting a new life in a new country for they came from a tradition in which it was common for people to travel for work. Workers from the Caribbean can be found all over the Americas. What hit them was the racism and the emptiness of the self-proclaimed probity of British Society. Black people had sacrificed their lives for the empire and the anti-fascist struggle urged on by colonial wartime propaganda. They expected the same sacrifice in return or at least some of the British fair play and decency they had heard so much about. They were to be betrayed. In their daily lives they were to find out that if these attributes were at play; the rules of the game had been altered because they were Black.

> We had to find accommodation and some of the notices read **'no coloureds, no Irish, no dogs.'** One woman actually spat in my face in Earl's Court. From you were Black you were out. People did not see a Black person as a businessman, manager or foreman but someone prepared to use the broom all their life. (Mr. Baker in the film 'From you were Black, you were out')

Mr. Baker arrived in Britain in 1944 to join the Royal Air Force. His humiliating experience was not unique. He had stayed on after the war. As an officer of an association for the welfare of workers from the Caribbean, he received a telegram notifying the arrival of the Empire Windrush in 1947. He made his way to the colonial office to enquire about the arrangements to welcome and settle them.

> I met one Major Keith and told him, these people are coming, no one to meet them, no where to go. You got homes for the Germans who bombed and killed us. Find homes for these people too.

Some provision was made for temporary accommodation but the lack of coherent policy on Black settlement led to the concentration of the arrivants in decaying inner city areas. This accentuated working class racism and led to physical attacks on Black families. In 1958 the so-called race riots broke out as the Black Community defended itself against local bigotry and the fascist bully boys of Sir Oswald Mosley.
☐

Recently a friend showed me (KO) some photos of gravestones in the war cemetery of Chittagong in Bangladesh. Many of them bore African names and they were of soldiers who sacrificed their lives for the British Empire and the fight against fascism. Chittagong was the site during the war of the major struggle between the British and Japanese empires. Not many relatives, family or friends in West Africa would know that their dear ones lay in this far flung cemetery, nor I suspect ever been told of the heroic role they played in halting fascism.

They may have received a telegram announcing they were missing, dead or feared dead. Those who came back had to wait till independence, a decade or so later, to raise a flame of remembrance to the unknown soldier. In the intevening years many of them, unemployed and living on the edges of poverty had to organise and fight for war indemnities and pensions. Ex-servicemen in the Caribbean and Asia went through similar experiences. The Colonial System was in crisis. There was mass unemployment and political turmoil and some colonial workers saw migration as a way of escaping from the period of depression.

In Notting Hill Gate the arrivants carved a home for themselves out of the sprawling urban landscape. Networks and landmarks of friendship and Community gradually took shape as people gave a helping hand to each other and came together to socialise and share common experiences. Notting Hill and the Grove became home and home is always where the action is.

For some, home was a cold basement and an unscrupulous landlord. Occasionally it was the abandoned room on the third floor with no electricity. In whatever situation they found themselves in they proved adoptive to the new environment, informing structures of mutual support with the spirit of social solidarity. A small family prayer meeting opened its doors to community fellowship. Working colleagues, relatives and friends came together in the traditional system of savings, the pardner or sousou. An appointed banker received weekly or monthly contributions from members and paid out lump sums of money in a rotating circle.

Padner supplemented incomes and facilitated the social accummulation and circulation of capital within the Community. It was particularly useful in raising mortgages. Many families were able to buy properties in the local area and develop them. Some of these properties were pulled to the ground in the 70's after a GLC Compulsory purchase order. A commendable feature of Padner is that it dispenses with masses of paper work which even small financial institutions find essential. It also contextualises the accummulation of personal capital within reciprocal social relations. The tradition goes back a long way; to the Caribbean and to the self-help societies of precolonial Africa.

50 Shops specialising in African foods opened on local streets, complemented here and there by bars and restaurants. Mangrove restaurant opened on All Saints road taking over from the Rio and Fiesta One. The youth came to places like Metro, Tabernacle and Acklam Hall to socialise and give cultural expression to the Black working class experience. The emergence of a Community reinforced Black cultural forms like Blues sessions and parties. These came into conflict with prevailing norms of entertainment and the law. As early as the 50's people like Duke Vine and Count Suckle had carved names for themselves as sound system operators in the area, playing at basement sessions and parties.

For Black people such entertainment was crucial in the face of the undeclared but effective *colour bar* in white pubs and clubs. Few appropriate places could be found for these sessions popularly known as 'Blues'. They happened in front rooms as well as abandoned basements. Police raids occurred with predictable regularity. One brother has vivid memories:

> Wherever you come from, you had a feel for
> the music. The people dem didn't too care
> where you come from. Dem people didn't
> have a prejudice like island thing, you
> know. For the youth dem, it was just
> oneness. Like when you finish work in a
> factory on a friday night, this is where you
> go, Blues dance. All de doors close and
> sounds just a drop in you head. Its like
> a refuge still. It remind you of home, the feel of
> it. From Blues sessions a culture develop.
> I remember one on Winston Road, played by a brother
> called Jucklin. One night in 1963 the door just
> kick down and policeman just step in and you
> hear funny sound, sound system switch off.
> Dem just bust up de dance!
> We couldn't understand it. De older people dem
> did know because it happen to them.
> A couple of brethren get fling on police van
> and get charge with obstructing police officers
> on de Monday morning. (From the film 'From you were Black you
> were out')

Blues dance is walking on the edge of Babylon and claiming cultural space. Black youth articulate their experiences and forge alternative aesthetics in opposition to dominant culture. On a winter's night when the moon is frozen and chill breeze take a walk, music drop from sound system like heavy lead. Dub voices chant all de while shaking the roof in full charge. The youth dance in combat formation, back to the wall and forward motion only. They've come from all over the Grove and beyond; for this is a vigil of testimony and incantation

J. ROSS

FITZROY SANG

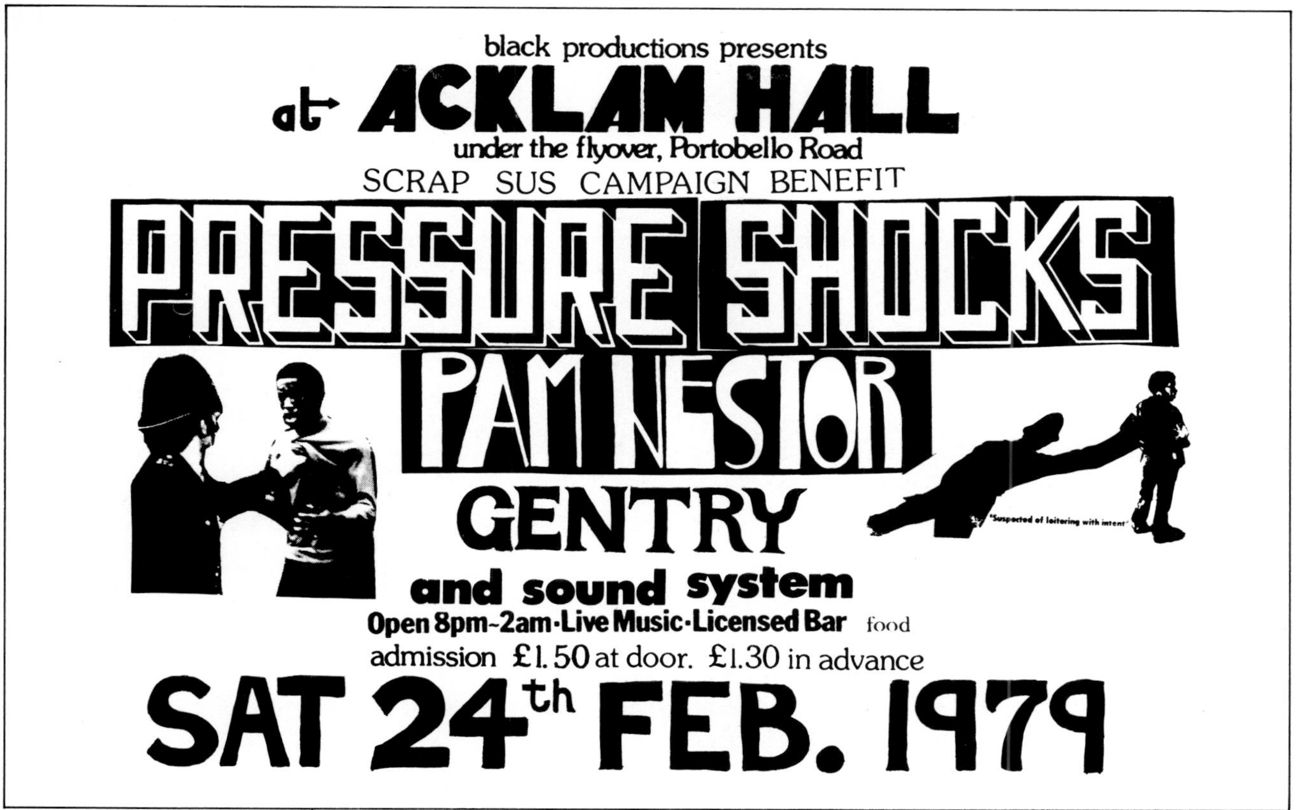

black productions presents

at **ACKLAM HALL**

under the flyover, Portobello Road

SCRAP SUS CAMPAIGN BENEFIT

PRESSURE SHOCKS
PAM NESTOR
GENTRY
and sound system

Open 8pm~2am·Live Music·Licensed Bar food

admission £1.50 at door. £1.30 in advance

SAT 24th FEB. 1979

"Suspected of loitering with intent"

threaded through Reggae rhythms. The trumpets take a turn and they come with force. The sounds, dub wise, jus stretch big and broad. A mellow guitar groove wails through waves of drums. It's an Aswad song. 'African Children' and the youth like it. They raise their prime fingers to the Dee Jay who lifts up Brinsley Forde's voice

De tribulation is so sad
De environment is so bad
Highrise concrete no backyard for de children to play
African children . . .
Concrete cubicles
De rent increases every other day
Essential repairs assessed but never done
And when it rains de children can't go out to play . . .
African children living in a concrete situation
African children.

Voices saturate the cramped basement and rise with the morning mist. The people here are below ground level and socially they occupy strategic locations for all of society is within scope. There are few real opportunities for the youth to fulfil their potential in Babylon so they walk the edge of downpression and focus their visions beyond the dreadlines of the night. Seeds of hope grow in their hearts and the Dee Jay chats with a fresh surge of melody. She tells them they should be ready for the eventual ritual of reckoning. 'De wicked a go drop like Twinkle Brothers dem say. See all Bagga Wire catch fire an' bubble up

53

de surface.' The echo chamber hits the words unto the concrete walls and the bounced sound, a receding thud races across the area.

Blues dance transcends mere cultural opposition. It is particularly significant for the ways in which Black Youth explore and create musical forms and textures using available technologies. Many sound systems own equipment they have partly constructed or adopted to suit their own needs. Speakers are built with appropriate wood to achieve desired sound densities. The sound chamber is made tight to maximise the sound output. A good speaker should be able to accommodate the bass line and drum calls and give them appropriate tone and resonance.

Some systems seperate out the sounds and channel them into individual speakers. It gives the Dee Jay a broader range of possibilities in the musical mix. Through decibel control and the use of effects s/he is able to desconstruct the sound elements, vacillate tone and texture and articulate them in a series of interactions. Over the years the often intense competition amongst sound systems has partly hinged on experimentation in musical styles and innovations in techniques of sound craft.

The microphone is the symbol of dialogue. The Dee Jay engages the past and present simultaneously, livening up the session with varying delivery styles and subjects. The Blues dance is a school of social and political education and everyone comes with something to give and take away. They come for a communal affirmation of their own personal experience and they celebrate with spirited choruses when the Dee Jay calls.

The history of the sound system in Britain has produced many styles and forms popularised by two generations of Dee Jays and sounds. They include Coxsone Outernational, Unity, Sir Lloyd, Turbo Supreme, People's War, Channel One High Power, King Tubby's HiFi, Saxon, Sister Culcha, Lorna Gee, Smiley Culture, Ranking Ann, Pato Banton, Mad Professor, Asher Senator, Sister Audrey, Macka B, Martin Glynn and Tippa Irie. The Dee Jay tradition echoes that of the Calypsonian and hip hop rapper. Historically they are all rooted in the role and function of the African griot as the eyes and ears of the community.

The Blues dance was complemented by weddings, parties and other social events. Working people came to Seymour and Porchester Halls, in their best, to enjoy themselves, reminisce Caribbean experiences and contemplate the fate of their sun lit dreams. When the band strikes mento, Ska or the other uptempo beats of an explorative generation, the floor fills up very quickly. Bodies move to the insistent rhythms and the hand that is strained by the machine grip loosens up to clusters of sounds and movements.

On such occasions there is always the lone person, alone with their memories in the midst of the jam. Brigades of voices roar with the heat

King Sounds & The Isralites

CARNIVAL 78

FRI 11th AUGUST

black productions presents
at **acklam hall**
under the flyover,
Portobello Road

SONS OF JAH

MAT STAGGER prag VEC

Open 8pm–2am
Licensed Bar
Live Music
admission £1.50

969 4329

and brisk feet but the lone figure sits in their own world of silence and meditation. You could say the music was sometimes almost unkind because when it grows on a person in a particularly low down groove, a home left in the sun assumes more than vivid imagery.

The 1950's and 60's was significant for the impact of Black culture on British Culture generally. The influence of Black music on youth and popular culture is particularly interesting. Each home prided itself with a record spinner and collections of records, some from relatives and friends from all over the African diaspora. On hot summer days the old gramaphones sat pretty on window panes or front room coffee tables and played ceaselessly. The popular musics were Ska, Mento, Calypso, Blues and Soul and later on Reggae. For White British youth they were points of entry into Black Culture, as well as an exploration of alternative cultural tastes. These musics fired imagination, bred curiosity and set off trains of fashion, social identities and attitudes. Out of Rock and Roll, Chuck Berry, Little Richard and others emerged the Teddy Boys. Soul Boys and their numerous cults closely followed the fortunes of Rhythm and Blues and Soul Singers — Wilson Pickett, Otis Redding, Sam Cooke, Sam and Dave amongst others.

These trends in post war white working class culture significant as they were, were largely influenced by an interpretation of black musicality and culture which hinged on racist stereotypes and patronage. The association of Black Music with hedonism and the primitive essence, for example circumscribed its overall aesthetic impact and denigrated the status of Black musicians. Most were merely seen as exotic entertainers. The failure to tackle racism in white youth culture led to acute socio-political ironies, not least of all the spectacle of Teddy Boy mobs physically attacking Black people in Notting Hill.

Jazz has longer historical precedents. As a popular form it followed the success of ragtime during the opening decades of the century. Ragtime was of course no more than modified ministrelsy, a racist musical form highly popular with white audiences. The precedents of Jazz set the tone for its consumption and exploitation and the framework for its interpretation. Invariably early jazz relied heavily on the image of the jazz musician as 'Uncle Tom' and carefree hedonist who catered for the escapist fantasies of white people. Most of the titles of popular jazz tunes could not be more appropriate to the racist discourse — 'Why do ya roll those yes,' 'Heart of a nigger' 'Jigs and Wigs', and 'You all look alike'. (Grateful to information from M. West's unpublished thesis, Black Rhythm and British Reserve: Interpretations of Black musicality in British Racist Ideology since 1750.)

Record Companies like Columbia and Parlaphone were to invest and exploit the commercial possibilities of the music and import US releases to an ever enlarging circle of enthusiasts. During the inter-war years musicians like Louis Armstrong, Duke Ellington and Carl Calloway were to tour the country and play to enthusiastic audiences.

The arrival of African soldiers in the U.S. Army in Britain, during the war gave jazz a big boost, as off-duty servicemen doubled as musicians. Many clubs opened in the West End, among them the West Club, Shim Sham, the Blue Lagoon and the Rhythm Club. These clubs gave to jazz a popular appeal but its immense potential was circumscribed by prevailing attitudes and politics. The location of these clubs, most of them in Soho, tied in quite well with stereotypical images of Black musicians and shady night-life and many fans visited them to 'have a feel of Harlem' and the ghetto.

White promotion of the music and musicians tended to appropriate the tradition for commercial gain with little acknowledgement of its history of African resistance in the US of A. Its social and political re-amifications were de-emphasised for exotica. It was simply the gas that filled the cylinders of West End hedonism. The image of the jazz musicians was predominantly that of comics, drug suspended kites of the ghetto and that of tragic heroes and heroines.

The arrival of Black workers from the Caribbean changed the context for jazz appreciation, instilling a much needed realism into it and challenging many of the preconceived expectations. It introduced a

J. ROSS

greater diversity of Black musical tastes and shifted the emphasis away from Soho to other parts of the city. The isolation of jazz musicians was also broken as they met and collaborated with the new arrivants. The cumulative impact of Black Culture on British Society proved considerable. The post war period crystallised earlier developments and gave them definite forms and social effectiveness. It gave to British society new conceptions of living, new tastes in food, and fashion.

John Millington, a veteran artist of Notting Hill who passed away recently was a young man in those days. He recollects the efforts of the arrivants to maintain their own tastes in dress and fashion and the impact this had on British Society.

> English trousers never fit well
> They had big waists which you
> hold with belts or braces. The
> jackets — well we make do with them
> but they always cover the trousers.
> You know we wear trousers to show it off
> To solve all dem problem we get our
> special cuts from Bourge's in the East End.
> Bourge's zoot trouser's really nice.
> When we step out everyone just turn and
> look. Some of the brothers even import
> trilby hats from Czechosolovakia. Those
> who don't like hat, roll them hair like
> Wilson Pickett. Very soon everyone want
> look like us. Its we who stop big man
> wearing school brazier in dis town. ☐

Mum, here comes the bulldozer

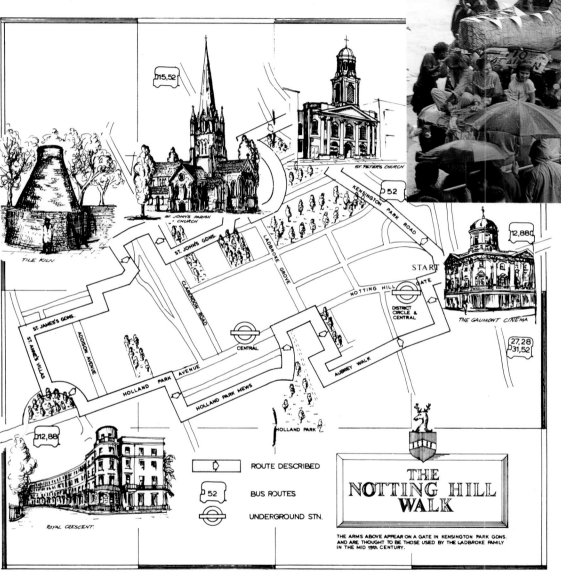

Like most areas in Greater London, Notting Hill has undergone significant changes ever since it evolved into an urban centre. It is so called after the tall gates that stood on the main London-Bath road before they were dismantled in 1864. In the 17th century a village evolved in the area due to the existence of gravel workings. Apparently nothing remains of this village today. Most of the area's infrastructure belongs to the 19th century and redevelopments of the 20th century.

The modern evolution of Notting Hill Gate has a lot to do with the evolution of industrial capitalism itself; particularly the need to provide the centres of production and commerce with a labour force. This labour force — originally expelled from the countryside by the cumulative effects of the Land Enclosure Acts and the privitisation of land — had settled in Central London. Between 1830 and 1880 however, it was forcibly evicted to make room for the expanding business infrastructure of the city and commercial premises. The authorities got away with paying little or no compensation.

> 'Despite the Metropolitan Street Improvement Acts of 1872 and 1877 which gave the Board of Works limited rehousing responsibilities, the Board continued to avoid these at all costs and the norm was compensation of £150 and week's notice... It had been estimated that street clearance and urban improvement alone evicted 100,000 people from Central London' (J. O'Mally, The Politics of Community Action, 1977).

Many of the people expelled from Central London moved to adjacent areas including Notting Hill. To facilitate the movement of workers from these areas to Central London, existing railway networks were expanded. The Great Western Railway was opened in 1838, due west out of Paddington, passing through the northern tip of North Kensington. The Metropolitan railway reached Hammersmith in 1869 and the Central Line was completed in 1899. Cheap fares were introduced in the 1860's. Some of the first working class houses in Notting Hill were in fact artisan cottages built to accommodate the workers who constructed the railways. As a result of these changes, workers in North Kensington were within a half-hour's journey to places of work in Central London. The capitalists had also succeeded in re-structuring yet again the spatial composition and character of the capital, affirming labour's subordination to the whims of profit, re-enforcing the landmarks and symbols of bourgeois life in the process.

By 1900, private landlords had built up most of North Kensington. Since then, their interests have not been fundamentally threatened either by the people, the local authority or housing trusts. A series of rent acts have served as a balancing mechanism regulating their powers to maximise profits through property speculation and attempting to give tenants a greater security of tenure.

The 1957 Act attempted the latter whilst the 1965 Act put paid to the era of landlord intimidation and gangsterism highlighted by the activities of Peter Rachman in the 50's and early 60's. Middle class landlords and property developers well-connected to the institutions of power have, generally speaking, taken these acts in their stride, re-interpreting the small print to suit their business objectives. Property owners for example, responded to the generally pro-poor tenant act of 1965 by switching their attention to high-income tenants or buyers, as the source of maximum profits likely to evade legislative controls. Today they provide the bulk of housing in Notting Hill. Council accommodation has increased from the mid-1960s when Kensington and Chelsea — one of the richest Inner City boroughs — had a stock of a mere 5,381 dwellings. Southwark, on the other hand, had 922,391 (1966).

Black People faced discrimination in the allocation of these council dwellings. This was effected mainly through racist assessment procedures and the application of housing criteria. It had the effect of over-concentrating Black tenants in run-down private dwellings. The authorities came to favour demolition and dispersal of affected residents as the solution. This was the end result of a vicious circle of social neglect and discrimination. Some Black families had spent their life savings to improve some of these properties, having been conned into illegal ownership by property dealers. They received little or no compensation. Many were rehoused in the high rise estates of White City, Hackney and as far away as the Isle of Dogs.

The dispersals split the community and destroyed many of the networks and structures of mutual support, nurtured over the past decades of settlement.

Mum, here comes the bulldozers. It's early morning and sun catches the big balls of steel slamming their way through concrete, shattering everything in their way. Everyone is going to White City. Dad has hired a van for the furniture and the kitchen ware. The children will go by bus or train. No one asked the council about how to get there; otherwise, it may have come up with day passes.

Cousin wants to come in the evening to fit the curtains. Mum doesn't really see the point. What use, she wonders, on the 14th floor. They would only cover the clouds. If the stars are allowed in they may perhaps, spark a dream or two. Something more problematic occupies her mind. The pardner banker now lives in Hackney. How is she going to make her weekly contributions if he can't come all the way to White City? A clever daughter suggests the post would do as if the faces on British stamps ever smile. She cuts her eyes because she knows she will need to call each of the thirty odd people in the pardner circle to find out how they are doing.

Mrs. Johnson suffers from arthritis and can barely stand the cold. It's a disaster when the lifts break down because she just cannot walk up ten floors. She sits in front of it, waiting and waiting. She can't call the council because all the telephones on the estate have been vandalised. Lost in her memories she starts incantating, calling the names of family and guiding spirits. The kids skate noisely around her. Mum's lucky locket is still hanging from her neck and she holds it tight. When flashes of youth touch her eyes, they fill it with tears.

J. ROSS

CARNIVAL VOICES

Leslee Wills is a textile designer who has worked closely with the Notting Hill Carnival movement since 1975. She is a member of Lion Youth Mas and together with Betty Campbell founders of Damara Marketing, an interior design and furnishing enterprise. Her work reflects a creative synthesis between the varying styles and techniques of the Carnival tradition and her own artistic development. Here she explores aspects of this synthesis and developments in the Carnival movement.

Tell us how you started

There was no starting point in my creativity because of the environment I was brought up in. I was born on All Saints Road in Notting Hill and grew up in Guyana, in a climate in which our cultural heritage was paramount in the consciousness of people. After Independence many people were also involved in rejecting western aesthetics. My childhood involved being able to appreciate African festivals. Guyana was then very much involved in investigating her own past. I remember going to Indian festivals and participating in them. There was also a spate of Black American Literature which influenced many people. I personally knew Rosa Guy because there were Caribbean writers and artists groups.

Coming back to England I got involved in the Black Community Supplementary Schools to teach History and English. This was at George Padmore and William Sylvester Schools in Finsbury Park, on a voluntary basis. I met many people not least of all Betty Campbell who taught in another school in the area. She was very much into textiles. I never saw myself as an artist at the time. I was artistic because I liked designing and fashion and a rebel because I knew I didn't want to do Law. Betty was also involved with Carnival and asked me to join her. I went along and from day one we became the designers for Sukuya Mas. Sukuya was very much into our African past and we did the designs. This was in 1975. People really felt the need to look authentically African on Carnival day and as you can imagine we were under considerable pressure if the costumes looked Guyanese, South American or vaguely European. You cried and went home and did more research to eventually come up with the right costume design. Your real assessors were your own peer groups and people in Carnival. You were not really answerable to the White world out there. You had to come up with something authentic and contrasting to our everyday lives. It was not easy but this was what we had to do in 1975.

J. ROSS

Tell us more about your experience as a Carnival designer

As a Carnival designer you always have to be willing to change and adopt to the moods and demands of the band and the dominant themes of the time. I mean, its no point thinking you would always play a theme you personally like. You've got to play especially to the young people, those with fresh ideas and energies. This is the only way the band survives. The younger people who do not have so many commitments also do a lot of the groundwork and you have to reflect their moods and styles. It usually works out very well.

Two or three years with Sukuya however revealed to us a particularly Trinidadian chauvinist element in Carnival. This involved the failure to understand any kind of mood or dynamic outside of Trinidad. Sometimes it meant all gloss and glitter at the same time. As a result of disagreements with the music section and the men who ran the band at the time, we broke off to form our own band. In 1976 saw the first all woman Carnival band. We called it The Lion Youth Carnival Band after Lion of Judah. There were about thirty women. We came out in 1977, from the Community in Finsbury Park and since then we've grown from strength to strength. We eventually incorporated men and a mobile sound system and stuck to our African themes.

Your involvement with Sukuya seems memorable

Yes, one of the positive dynamics then was that it was a time Carnival really affirmed its African roots. There were people like Larry Ford, Ken Morris, Arthur Peters, Merle Majors, Rauf Webster and many others at Mangrove who stuck fiercely to the notion of the African past and were not going to be swayed from it. People produced beautiful sculpture from their own experience and from historical reconstructions. Ken Morris was well known for his papier marché figures and huge masks. We did the designs for the costumes and they did the three dimensional pieces to go with them. By emphasising African themes we were in a sense moving away from the 'Butterfly tradition.'

The Butterfly tradition

You know, Peter Minshall king of thing, wings, bats, being pretty and almost acceptably European. Once Trinidad had reached that stage; touristic and acceptable, they just stuck there. Another memorable experience was when we claimed an old and abandoned school on Harrow road for ourselves. We built printing tables and set them up in the science labs and used old equipment in the school to do our casting and so on. All the time we did not realise how revolutionary it was, to take over public property to create popular art and cater for so many people. We just got on with it and did it. That was positive. We were willing to go through any sacrifice for Carnival. Developing a strong commitment is part of the spirit of Carnival. That really puts you in good stead later on because if you could design and take on all the various complaints, criticisms of the community in Notting Hill, I think you could do it anywhere else.

Tell us a bit more about your struggle to affirm the African past. How did you go about doing it

Lion Youth emerged out of the George Padmore and William Sylvester schools which was very much involved in teaching African history and culture. This connection was important. It also made it possible to reach more younger people who perhaps liked modern themes. When they decide to have a theme of gold and silver, we have the Egyptians and the Nubians. When they decided to do wings, a fantasy mas, we investigated the Saramacans from Paramarago in Surinam; slaves who thought they could fly back to Africa. In these ways we created mas which were not only relevant but also firmly rooted in our traditions. Once a theme has been chosen different people in the band investigate different possibilities in terms of the construction of the mas. Its a collaborative effort.

What considerations go into choosing a theme

Many things but I suppose the practicality of the idea, whether it can be done. Nobody gets very excited anymore until they have thought out very clearly in their own mind exactly where the materials for the costumes are going to come from, the colours they want and how they are going to construct it. Not how they are going to decorate it. Experience has shown that what is crucial is how a costume is going to be constructed and worn. Decoration is easily organised later on. This is one of the reasons why we have a design team now. You might be very gifted in sewing lovely suits but if you can't construct a 'mummy water' figure so that she stands tall, twelve foot in the sky, you just don't do 'mummy water'. And once you've built it in a room, how does it come out. When ideas are put out in groupsessions, we put our heads together and invariably choose one. We don't fight over ideas. Last year we did Hannibal. Some of us had noticed the work of Donald Rodney at the Black Art Gallery. He had a method of constructing head pieces which were light and able to be carried easily. From my work at the Commonwealth Institute I also knew they had African elephant heads we could use as moulds. These ideas were discussed, pushed in different directions and developed. Once you've decided on a theme, your judge is not the market place because you are not producing commodities. They are your fellow band members so we develop the highest standards. Most band members have been involved for ten years now.

Who provides the music for the band

We work with a local mobile sound system called switchcraft. They come with us on a lorry that has a platform for speakers and specially constructed tapaulin. Its much difficult to organise the logistics than

most people think. There is the question of spare generators which need to be carried along because everything stops when the music stops. In the past we had members who were also with a Brazilian dance group. They came with drums if the theme needed drumming.

What about Damara textiles, how does your involvement in Carnival inform your work as a designer

Involvement with Carnival gives you the opportunity to push yourself to the out-most in this environment. At Arts College they tried to take away my Carnival experience and habits. They tried to break me but they failed and failed again. I just continued to produce and document. Whether they liked it or not, I had the goods and there were people responding to them. Researching for Carnival also exposes you to a broad spectrum of ideas, many of which are not easily available.

Your last exhibition at Black Art Gallery was called Palenque. Tell us about it

Palengue was an escaped slave settlement on the borders of Guyana and Brazil. Its the equivalent of the Moroon Settlements in Jamaica. In this settlement African Slaves recreated their own historical traditions as they remembered them. Essentially they cut themselves off from the pressures to be absorbed. Palengue occurred to me because that is what many people are trying to do here. Its not an easy fight. For one thing there is the problem of the overseer mentality. In the Caribbean it is the ex-slave who sells the others down the river. In Britain today they want to build a whole class of overseers to police everyone else. They make it difficult for you, always tempting you to join them. Everytime you wake up you have to remind yourself there are certain things you just wouldn't do. Palengue is just my idea describing a state of mind, of the past we have to tread to keep our own ethics, beliefs in ourselves and our past whilst going through the rites of passage into Britain. □

J. ROSS

David Rudder is now one of the foremost Calypsonians in Trinidad. In 1986 he was crowned Calypso Monarch and won the King of the Road March title. His song 'Bahia Girl' and 'Hammer' were road favourites. Here he talks about his life and work and new developments in Trinidadian music and culture.

David Rudder — Calypsonian

I started singing in 1965. You know, cover versions of Temptations, Four Tops, Marvin Gaye, Stevie Wonder and the other Motown greats. Then in 1970 I started writing my own songs. It's also around the same time that I got into Soca music. I have been doing that since then. Initially there were five of us in the singing group which employed a backing band. I have been working with 'Roots' my present band for five years. We specifically formed it to play Calpyso and Soca music because there weren't many bands in Trinidad then doing that. Most of them were variety bands playing all types of music.

How do you place yourself in relation to the other Calypsonians

As musicians with varying experiences we inevitably produce varying sounds. I also have my own ideas about song writing, style and so on. The past informs my work a great deal and I use it as a catalyst for the future. Our songs are very old but we present them to people as something new.

Like Sparrow. Kitchener and the others

Sparrow is tops. He is in a class of his own. Kitchener also. They are forerunners of an old African tradition. If you check it much of African history was passed down from generation to generation orally and Calypso is a continuation of that tradition. Today its effectiveness can be quite interesting. Recently the wife of King Edward who abdicated the English throne died. The radio in Trinidad played a calypso someone sung when he abducated. The song went 'its love, its love alone that caused King Edward to leave his throne.' If you do not know when Edward abdicated the throne, you can place the event within the historical context of the song.

How do you relate the oral tradition to your song writing

My songs are usually culturally oriented. 'Bahia Girl' is for example not just a story of boy meets girl. Its also a story about the marriage of the strong Yoruba tradition in Trinidad and Bahia. We use a simple love story to celebrate the survival of African traditions in the Caribbean and South America. It acknowledges the link between Trinidadian and Brazilian cultures and a recognition of a common background which is Ile Ife, which is Africa. The song might seem simple on one hand but most of my songs have other levels. The rhythms also relate to what I am trying to say culturally. There is a bit of Soca, Samba, Shango and

Calypso. In fact all the seperated elements of the African experience come together in the song. It is therefore talking to the soul of the people at different levels.

'Bahia Girl' became a hit everywhere. How do you access its impact in Trinidad

Initial responses were fairly mixed. There were those who liked it and of course those who saw me as a threat in the Calypso world. They criticised the song saying it was not 'heavy' enough. Then a strange thing happened. The Brazillian Embassy wrote an article in a Trinidadian paper on the significance of the song. The Nigerian Embassy also contacted me. You check what was happening? They knew what it was all about. We didn't and it was because we were forgetting those elements of our history and traditions which inform us as a people. The song reminded people of those elements and it hit them.

Why do you think there is this historical forgetfulness in Trinidad

Well, we have been distracted a lot over the last ten years. We have had a lot of oil money flowing into the country. This money has come with its own imported values which have distracted us as a people. For one thing we became very Americanised. As Third World people we absorbed a lot of the negative elements of US Culture. Right now oil is not such a big thing in Trinidad and society is kind of sobering up or levelling off. This is increasingly being reflected in the music.

How did this Americanization affect Carnival

Carnival became a bit more commercialised. You see Carnival is really an occasion for social commentary and artistic expression. People make statements which come out of the conditions of their daily lives. The rejected of the society used that day to vent their feelings. In South America there was even a Government that was overthrown on Carnival Day. There are now Carnival festivities all over the world, New York, Boston, Toronto, Montreal, Detroit, Los Angeles, London . . . with time they may become even more commercialised. But you know inside of everything there are always people making statements. In Trinidad Carnival will become more hard-edged if Society falls to such levels of decadence. But the last ten years has really been a period of relative economic stability and calm.

Increased commercialisation affects creativity

Well, if you have lots of money, you could make very expensive costumes. But those who don't have it are very resourceful. They sustain the dynamism of Carnival. When things are hard people get very ingenious. They even use dried bread collected from bakeries.

Calypsonian: Arrow

J. ROSS

They paint them and decorate them. You would not believe it if someone told you what it was. The process brings out the skill in people. But you know those who want to play big mas will always play big mas because it relates to their own life styles and psychologies.

What about your own involvement

I got involved in Carnival in 1973. I worked with Ken Morris, one of the veterans of Carnival. He worked in copper and other metals and produced some startling sculpture. We used to design costumes and pictures for his band. We enjoyed those days very much. It was about releasing yourself and sponteneity was important. In Carnival things do not always go as planned and the event always gives itself a certain degree of free play. I remember a Peter Minshell mass called 'The River'. Everyone was painted white and at a certain stage in front of everyone, they were supposed to apply some dyes and change colours. But there was a long frustrated wait to get to the stage area and people just got a bit impatient and started using the dyes. They looked like mud afterwards. You see, you can't programme people or choreograph their movements and intentions. They always say to themselves this is our festival and if we feel to do something now, we do it.

How did you see your intervention in Calypso presently

The last ten years has seen a kind of musical synthesis in Trinidad. We have the legacy of soul music from the sixties. The seventies was a period of political upheaval with people looking into themselves a bit more than they did. The hybrid of Soca, a continuation of Soul and Calypso occured when people started experimenting more. What has however happened since then is that Soca has graduated to a point where there is more soul or disco pop than Calypso. What I am trying to do is to go in the opposite direction and place the music firmly in its historical roots. □

LEATHERCRAFT
BEN ALLEYNE

SILKSCREEN PRINTING
TURU POMEL

Carnival Industrial Project is a Community resouce and training centre based in Notting Hill. It provides space and facilities for Carnival groups and organisation and enables them to build floats, steelpans and costumes and make tee-shirts. It is one of the few projects which has the facilities for an all year round preparation for Carnival. Nonetheless it has been plagued by unreliable funding and local council support. Victor Crichlow, the Manager is a veteran of the Carnival movement. This brief interview looks at his involvement in Carnival and the project.

Victor Chrichlow

My memories of Carnival go back a long way to Trinidad. Here in Britain my involvement begun with the disguise competition, the forerunner to the costume competition. People literally disguised themselves playing different characters and themes. I won the first one as a king sailor, portraying the Eiffel Tower. Claudia Jones, then the proprietor of West Indian Gazette used to organise the competitions. From then on my involvement got deeper and deeper. I organised the first king of bands competition at Hammersmith and other shows at Rochester Hall and other venues in the area. I was invited to join the Carnival Committee around 1972. Leslie Palmer was then in the chair.

When did the idea for the Carnival Industrial Project come up

As you know there was a movement to stop the Carnival around 1975. This became very apparent in 1976. We fought against it and won. One of the lessons we learnt from that struggle was that we had to organise to ensure the continuity and permanency of the event. The tradition had to be passed on to the youngsters born here. Making a costume is a process which demands many skills — leather craft, silkscreen, painting, designing, wire-bending etc. We needed a project to teach these skills and CIP grew out of this need. We wanted to establish an infrastructure to keep the Carnival tradition alive.

When did the project start

1979. Initially we wanted a purpose built building but the Council did not come up with sufficient funding. We had to make do with a porter cabin. The people in the Community actually put it together. Training started in 1982. Most of the banners you see at Carnival, tee-shirts, are made here. Bands use our facilities to make costumes, foot wear, and flots. We also supply steel pans and related accessories. We have also been working in schools to popularise the steel pan tradition. We want people to see the steel pan as an instrument they can play all year round and not just at Carnival time.

Who funds you

We get some support from the Manpower Services under the Youth

Opportunities Programme (YOP) which changed to Youth Training Scheme (YTS). This year (1986) they changed it to Youth Training Scheme 2. The problem is that whenever they change the programme it affects the funding arrangements. Some of the arrangements do not necessarily suit voluntary organisations. We have not been funded this year. We went to our Council, Kensington and Chelsea for deficit funding but nothing was forthcoming. Presently we are in the process of changing our focus on training to a more varied commercial venture. We do not intend to stop our training programme but we need to generate our own funds to be self-sufficient. There is of course, a role for funding agencies in this crucial project. CIP is a community venture with a management committee made up of local organisations. It provides a permanent space for the processes which go into the making of Carnival. Its a link and a focus for the development of the skills which we need to pass on from generation to generation. □

Cello-pan
This is next in tone range to the Bass. It is similar in appearance, but rather shorter, and has a greater range of some 8 notes. Usually Cello-pans are played together in pairs to give the players a greater range and more scope for chording.

Guitar-pans
Also frequently played in pairs, Guitar-pans have a far greater range of up to 14 notes each.

Soprano-pan
The most versatile and magical instrument of all. Up to 8 inches deep, the Soprano has 28 different notes marked and tuned once it has been through the stretching and tempering process.

These are the basic instruments, but steelband makeup is infinitely variable, and any number of combinations are possible. This accounts for the many different types of steelband sound, and the very varied musical arrangements.

Some of the additional pans made at the **C.I.P.** workshops are **Double Seconds, Double Tenors, Tenor Bass, Echophones** and **Quadrophonics.**

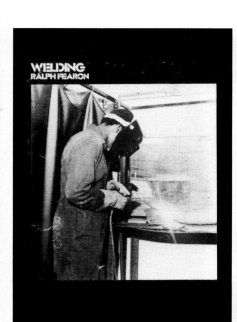

WELDING
RALPH FEARON

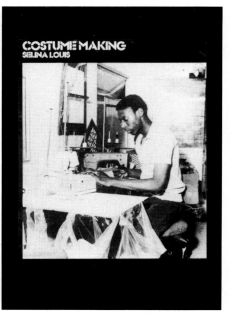

COSTUME MAKING
SELINA LOUIS

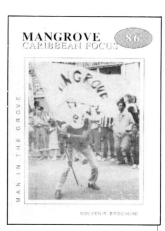

MANGROVE
CARIBBEAN FOCUS 86

MAN IN THE GROVE

SOUVENIR BROCHURE

Mangrove's spokesperson on Black community, struggle and Carnival.

Mangrove has been involved in local politics for a long time; ranging from Notting Hill Housing Trust, organisations like card and Tabernacle Community Centre. You also had, of course the Mangrove trial centred around the politics of the area. As Darcus Howe said in our magazine, Focus 86, the last time he spoke publicly, in the streets, he was arrested for it. The Mangrove trial raised the issue of policing in the area. Harassment and brutality of Black people were constant in the area.

Metro Youth Club also became an important focus for Mangrove. Initially ILEA had said it was going to renovate the old church building and hand it over to the community. They have not done this to this day. We were also involved in the development of the Notting Hill Housing Trust to ensure that Black people get a better deal in housing. There was a process of the gentrification of the area, with the white middle class moving in. They started moving Black people from the Colbern Square area and we had to campaign against that.

After the Mangrove trial we had two other trials at the Metro. The community was defended by an array of organisations. Black Peoples Information Centre, Grassroots, etc. One significant culmination of these developments was the emergence of Africa Liberation Day. It also enabled us to broaden out and link up with Black Organisations across the country.

There was the George Jackson Trust in Manchester headed by Ron Phillips, Harambee in Birmingham, Jimmy Rogers in Toxteth etc. We developed a network of support and solidarity. Carnival took much strength from this movement. Metro had the largest steel band because it had the facilities to build the pans etc. Mangrove helped tremendously in the early stages of Carnival. □

Lion Youth Mas — Community creativity in action.

Lion Youth is a carnival mas named after the 'Lion of Judah', Emperor Haile Sellassie of Ethiopia. As one of the established bands of Notting Hill Carnival it is known for its innovative expression of African themes and as one of the most spontaneous and exciting bands on the road. Joining a Lion Youth mas procession is an extra treat on Carnival Day. The emphasis is on communal celebration and the African inspired themes inform it with rich historical references which capture the intense moods of jollification.

Since 1977, when it first played mas till now, Lion Youth has given us a variety of original mas sometimes producing exceptional costumery and sculpture. These are created through collaborative processes which involve all members of the band. The organisation of the Band's output is also highly effective with the involvement of many women in positions of power and co-ordination. The first mas exploring Ethiopian culture produced some intricate designs based on traditional Ethiopian costumery. This was followed in 1978 by an interpretation of the life and career of Shaka, the great Zulu leader who resisted European colonialism in Southern Africa. *'Guerilla completing Shaka's Task'* was in the tradition of historical affirmation for contemporary practice. Shaka's task is clearly uncompleted. Playing the mas symbolised a rehearsal drama of remembrance. It brought the history of Southern Africa to the streets of Notting Hill and gave people the insights of struggle which inform the present fight against white minority rule in Azania (South Africa).

'Wings of Freedom' (1980) continued the themes of cultural resistance and historical documentation. This time the specific tradition explored was the Saramacans, a community of African Slaves in Surinam who believed they could fly back to their homeland in Africa. The band researched the legend to create mobile sculptures which emphasised the wings. It used innovative wire bending techniques to create huge wings strapped to the shoulders of the players.

'White Fowl, Drum and Candle' (1981) was one of their most successful mas. It delved into the elements of African religion, highlighting the common elements and articles used in the diverse but familiar practices in Africa and the Caribbean. The religious theme was elaborated in *Big Drum and Bongo*. The following year's mas depict the Caraca of Grenada and the Bongo dance from Trinidad. That same summer Lion Youth held its first children's carnival at the High View recreation centre in Islington.

'Egyptian Jamming' (1983) was a journey to the first civilization of the world; connecting and affirming its African roots and articulating its contemporary significance. The mas achieved a dignified profile of Black ancestral wisdom. The female section portrayed 'Cleopatra' and the male section 'Nubians' after the forerunners of the Egyptians. The children explored the themes of 'Tutankhamun boy king and Daughter

of Isis.

Lion Youth returned to a religious theme in 1985. *'Mammy Water'* the myth of the Sea Lady, half fish, half human who protects seafarers, sailors and fishing folk. The myth is popular on the West African Coast and in the Caribbean. Mas sections, assumed the local names of the Sea Lady. A 'Yemanja' to her worshippers in Bahia, Brazil and 'La Sirene' in Zaire.

'Grass Mas' ruled in 1985. It was inspired by the people of Badule of West Africa. Lion Youth created spectacular costumes and colourful masks to their memory. It followed this up with *'Hannibal Rules'* in 1986. Hannibal was a great general of the State of Carthage who conquered the Romans after a dramatic crossing of the Alps with a fleet of elephants. □

Members of Lion Youth talk about their work and involvement with Carnival.

Mrs. Sylvester

I should say I am the mother of Lion Youth. I have been the co-ordinator since we started, guiding developments, organising the children, reminding people of their responsibilities and getting everyone involved. I do a few other things, helping to prepare food for the Band, looking after guests and so on. And of course I play mas. Everyone in Lion Youth plays mas in addition to their other responsibilities.

I have seen Lion Youth grow bigger and bigger over the years. My best mas was *'White Fowl, Drum and Candle'*. I really enjoyed it. For me it was the highest point of Lion Youth mas. I was also fascinated by it because it made me remember my grandmother. She was a Shango woman back home in Grenada. My eldest brother was also very much involved in Carnival. He had a big band and always sang a song called 'Jaya ro'. My grandfather played mas on horseback. *'White Fowl, Drum and Candle'* brought home long memories of my family because Carnival goes back a long way for me. Most of my children play mas with Lion Youth. I like the historical themes very much.

Jean Gray

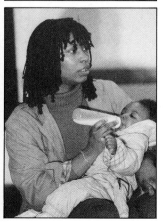

As part of the design team I am responsible for putting together ideas for the theme. First of all we have meetings to decide what we are going to play. We then go away and do some research and background work. We find pictures, photos, draw them, work on possible designs and bring the ideas back to the band. The costume designs are cut out on paper and tried out. The next stage is to find the right fabrics for the costumes. 'I'm afraid we always have to go for the cheap ones because of financial constraints. The sewer provides samples of the costumes and show them round. If everyone is happy

Karen   Debby

Victor   Sonia

Ann   Nikky

we go ahead and make the costumes. The important thing is to make sure you've got general consensus on the theme. But you know, people are so different in their styles that its not always possible to please everyone. Everyone wants their costume special. I have been involved in Carnival since 1976 and things have worked out very well.

Debby Enoe

I help with the sewing as part of the design team. I like it very much, shopping for materials which will suit the design. My best year was when we played *'Grass Mas'*. I helped with the designing.

Karen Enoe

I help with the children's Carnival. Last year we did a play called *'Hannibal rules'*. This took a lot of work out of us. I helped the kids with their costumes. I started in 1983 and my best mas was *'Mammy Water'*. I played queen in *'Hannibal Rules'*.

Victor Sylvester

Music comes out of Trinidad, the States and everywhere. I co-ordinate with the other members to buy the most popular tunes for Carnival day. Members of the band sometimes loan their records to the band. On the road the sound is crucial and we make sure we satisfy the people. The feeling you get playing mas is wonderful. I have also been involved with wire bending. I made some of the big wings for the *'Wings of Freedom'* mas. The thing about wire bending is that you have to move and bend with the wire. It breaks when you make it resist your force. I also do a lot of driving on Carnival day. People have to get to Notting Hill from the mas camp here in Finsbury Park. We hire about eight vans for that.

Sonia Brown

I am the assistant treasurer of the band. I help collect membership fees and balance the books. Fees are used to make the costumes, pay for transport, food and other accessories. We also get some funds from the Arts Council and Haringey Council. Parents also make donations to the children's Carnival. The money is never sufficient for the things we have to do but we always organise around what we get. That is why we always choose very cheap materials; not because we like cheap materials, its all we have money for.

What was your best Carnival?

O God so many. One of the best was when we played the *Arawaks* in 1979. It was full of fun. I also enjoyed *'White Fowl, Drum and Candle'* and *'Egyptian Jamming'*. The feeling you get on the road is something else. You don't need to drink, you are on a constant high. You really get into it and you forget all your sorrows (referring to baby, Doreen, You agree don't you.) I hope Carnival goes on for a long time because

it is one of those essential things for Black people in this country. We celebrate our 10th anniversary this year and we'll be planning lots of activities.

Tracy Sylvester

Over the years I have been helping out with the kiddies Carnival. On the day I organise the entertainment and games. I help dress the kids and walk up with them across Croach Hill. Last year I painted *'Hannibal Rules'* on a banner for them at the mas camp. I used to play mas with the kiddies when I was younger. I've also played in the men's section and wore a white shirt, white coat and turban, swords, shields, the lot. My best mas was *'Egyptian Jamming'*. It was all blue and nice. Strapless tops and plaited skirts, sash around our waists, head gear. . . *'Egyptian Jamming'* was great and I really enjoyed myself. □

Kiddies from Lion Youth Carnival Band

Wilf Walker is a music promoter and Carnival organiser. He has been responsible for all the fixed stages in Carnival since 1979. These have provided excellent audiences for many bands and groups. In 1981 he chaired the Carnival Arts Committee. Here he sketches his involvement as organiser and explains why he did not work on Carnival '86.

B. MARSDEN

Wilf Walker

In 1978 I asked Roger Markman who ran the North Kensington Amenity Trust to put up a stage for the bands. As you know a substantial part of Carnival happens on land owned by the trust. A commitment was made by the Council to make land available to the Community when the flyover was built. He built a platform about one foot high! That really was not good enough. The area bordering the junction of Acklam and Portobello roads is a focus for Carnival which attracts thousands of people.

What I had in mind was a prominent stage for all the major Black acts in the country. And I joined the Carnival Committee to help put that stage there. We did it and since then we've had staged performances as highlights of the event. The bands play on both days from morning till evening. We've had bands like King Sounds, Aswad, Eddy Grant, Gasper Lawal, Amazulu and numerous up and coming local bands. The problem of course is that all music has to stop at nine o'clock. Most of the people leave when we tell them the show is over, but on occasions it has not stopped the police charging in. Substantial police reserves are usually kept on the alert at Isaac Newton school and others in the area. At the appropriate time they charge towards each other squeezing everything in the middle.

J. ROSS

Things got better in the late 70's and early 80's.

Yes, mainly through our own efforts but we never got any credit for it. I remember a very senior police officer giving me a handshake in the dark after the successful Carnival of 1979. He could not see me and I could barely see him. Its always done in that kind of unofficial way. Your man here was central to the success but the officers most probably went and got all the accolades. I chaired the Carnival Committee in 1981. To my possible detriment I got my picture taken with police officers for the press saying we were going to work together and all that. This was half the truth because we were actually battling against all the odds to make the event happen. Essentially the police pay lip service to the community. You could discuss arrangements beforehand but find yourself renegotiating at Notting Hill Police Station on the very day of Carnival. When lines of communication start getting blurred, you know you are actually dealing with Scotland Yard and the Metropolitan Police and not the local officers you were negotiating with before. The organisation of the event suffers a lot because of this. And there is a lot of pressure on the organisers. I usually discuss arrangements for power for the PA systems well before hand but on the day we might be put in a situation where we have to get it from the flat of a guy across the road.

You did not work on the 86 Carnival.

Well I have done it for seven years and been used by the police and the British State at large. The Black Community gets ripped off over Carnival. It has become central to police credibility in terms of good race relations as well as the tourist industry in London. As trade begins to slump at the end of August here is a major event that takes it into September. Even if they gave us £¼ m that will still be small change in terms of the profits the state, London Transport, The Breweries etc. make on the street.

What do you think can be the real deal.

When the Black Community, at the end of the event, has enough money to finance its own arts and cultural activities for a year. The event is also now so big that in August we should be able to run Black events with Carnival themes in all the Theatre and Concert Halls in West London. Hammersmith, Palais and the Odean, Riverside, Commonwealth Institute, Acklam Hall, Tabernacle and all the other venues in the area. We also need some dignity for the artists. The financial aspect is just not right. We have been managing four stages with about seventy hands. They are selected from a total of about 120. Its really a huge task organising the equipment, personnel and schedules. The Carnival Committee gave me £1200 to do three months work, pay an assistant and two telephone bills. Its quite ridiculous because one GLC Concert used to cost anything around £1500.

I also feel that every musician who takes part in Carnival should at least be on the musicians union rate. Sometimes a band with as many as ten people get £50 or £100. In the past they used to get a case of beer each. I just cannot continue to condone this. Come the revolution I'll be shot. Carnival has also got a lot bigger. Most of the people who now come to it are white. If you check their involvement with the Black Community, Black Arts, The Black Liberation Struggle you'll find there is little interest. For many the attraction is that there is this event at which you can come to dance on the streets and do your thing.

How do you see the future

Carnival as an institution is here to stay and we need to resolve the issues I have raised. Also the business aspect of the event needs to be thoroughly organised. We need a business committee of the highest acumen. We have brothers and sisters in the community with excellent business and legal experience who should be brought together as a committee to negotiate with funding bodies, state institutions and business. We should mark off the Carnival area and negotiate all the possible deals in the area. The most senior of policemen would need to accept this committee and sit down with it to discuss logistics, crowd control, public facilities and so on. We should be privy to all the information so that we can really work together with the police. □

POSTSCRIPT 87

NO STOPPING US NOW!

A whole battalion can't stop a song
An announcement can't seize the surge in us
The road is for mas on Carnival day
So tell me 'what de hell police can do!'

A stadium can't hold a mas jam
For we are free spirits and more
Flying, tip toeing and dancing
In the open skies and sea and streets
So tell me 'what de hell the police can do!'

THE INDE

Daily

DAY 1 SEPTEM

Stabbed WPC a

Darknes
brings
fear to
streets

RIOT
AT C

LONDON

TANDARD

TONIGHT'S WEATHER CLOUDY

1 SEPTEMBER, 1987 20p

ss arrests in
b fury bring
l for action

BAN
THE
RIOT
CARNIVAL'

Carnival battle . . . Riot police tackle a young m

A TORY MP called on Home years in the wake of a bloody
Secretary Douglas Hurd to ban weekend.
Notting Hill Carnival in future

by Neal Harrison,
Gervase Webb, Paul
Cheston and Nigel
Bunyan

DAILY
Mirro

Tuesday, September 1, 1987   FORWARD WITH BRITAIN

33 hurt, 97 arrested in

CARNIV
RIOT CO
STORM

A POLICEWOMAN was among
33 people injured when riots
flared as the Notting Hill Carnival came to an abrupt and bitter
end last night.

A total of 97 people were arrested as
gangs of rampaging youths fought
pitched battles with police in the
streets.

More than 1,000 police wearing riot

Not
fun

20p

70 hurt in clashes

ERRO...
RNIVAL...

Phillips for m...

fu...

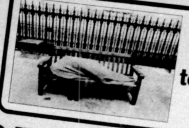

Now
stre
tempor
— centr

News Line

20p DAILY

Wednesday September 2, 1987

Number 3437

POLICE ATTAC
WAS PLANNE
—says Carnival organiser...

THE police attack at
the Notting Hill Car-
nival on...

The Daily Telegraph

FINAL*

DEREK
PYJAMAS
...for the
dressed s
SAVILE ROW

...AY SEPTEMBER 1, 1987   LONDON AND MANCHESTER   25p

THE LONDON EVENING STANDARD

Dancing with danger

STANDING BY . . . Riot police carrying shields and truncheons wait to quell trouble

Continued from Page I

going for 22 years but the
residents have been subjected
to terrible disruption let alone
the violence last night.

Leslie Curtis, chairman of
the Police Federation, said the
carnival had become a
battleground for people to
hammer the police.

He added "There has to be
very serious consideration by
all—including the Govern-
ment—whether this can carry
on on the streets.

"It has become an excuse
for theft and organised crime
and once it gets dark and
there is cover and shadows
bricks and stones get hurled
at the police.

"We are going to get the
same reaction from the car-

nival organisers that the
police over reacted. But what
do they want—dead poli-
cemen?"

Deputy Assistant Com-
missioner Paul Condon defended the police action in
sending in the riot forces.

"We had no option but to
put police into protective
equipment," he said.

"What could we do, let the
bottle throwing escalate or try
to intervene.

Black community leaders
angrily condemned the
violence.

Local community relations
officer Jimmy Barley warned:
"No serious West Indian
would let his wife and daughter on the streets now." The
carnival organisers faced not
only "white opposition" but

also conflict within their own
community from the older
generations, he said.

Mr Barley said "It started
as a traditional steel band
carnival ... now it is all
reggae and rastafarian music.
There is a terrible conflict
between the first generation
West Indians and the public
who started it and the younger
ones who run it now.

Mr Barley was reacting to
the demand by a police chief
that "society as a whole must
decide if the criminal side is
too high a price to pay for the
fun side."

Deputy Assistant Com-
missioner Paul Condon described the event as "un-
republised" and said "it
always caused concern from a
public safety and crime
aspect."

The violence was a blow for
the police who had reduced
their numbers from previous
years because the carnival
committee was providing 200
paid stewards for crowd
control.

Although 23-year-old Michael Galvin was grabbed to...

MOMENT OF TENSION — Police officers take away a
youth during the height of the trouble

Danny Holden, an executive
member of the organising
committee, stressed that...

Riot police
with mob
Notting H

By David Graves

THE NOTTING HILL carn
violence last night after r
broke out between riot poli
mobs in the Portobello Road m

Police barricaded all roads leading
hundreds of riot police, carrying sh
truncheons, cleared nearby street
charges.

Three injured officers,
including a Wpc, were
rushed to St Mary's Hospi-
tal, Paddington, after bottles
rained down in Acklam
Road.

Ninety-seven people were
arrested and about 60 people
were hurt.

By midnight most of the trouble had died down and the area
was quiet but tense.

Heavy-handed behaviour'

The violence was the worst at
the carnival since the riots in
the mid-seventies.

Groups of blacks in the area
claimed the police had started
the trouble by their "heavy-
handed" behaviour.

But a Scotland Yard spokes-
man angrily denied that police
had caused the violence.

He said ". . . mob of men vio-
lently turned on police in a
totally unprovoked series of
attacks using bricks and bottles.
We support carnival whole-
heartedly. Who on earth should
we stop things at the outset."

The trouble started about
9pm when gangs of youths, both
black and white, started hurling
bottles and beer cans at police
in Portobello Road.

Stalls were looted and over-
turned as police tried to break
up crowds.

Innocent bystanders

Spar
ho
chao

AIR TRA
at Barc
yesterday
ahead with
on Saturday
out further
agreement
their pa...

The conc
matter will
decide on fu...

At the
celled a me
last Saturda
signed betwe
the Transpo
aviation depa...

Back

But they
mind . . claim
gave up the
backpay to b...

A strike of
chaos and flig
20 hours to...

Barcelona se
Brava resorts

Barcelona
claim they...

Dunk
nks i...

**I am confident that it will continue and that the only
change will be that it will be extended — Alex Pascall,
Chair, Carnival Arts Committee.**

J. ROSS

organisers disappeared. Police countered Black insistence that the celebration remain in the streets with threats and more threats. As tension mounted, the Black Information Centre wrote letters to the Commissioner of Police, to the *Times* and *Guardian* newspapers and to local bodies, warning of an impending explosion. They pointed out that a combination of racist opposition by a vocal white minority, and the tightening of repressive methods of control by the police and local authorities, were leading to an explosion. Nothing happened.

From our own assessment of the situation, the attitude of the police clearly indicated that they thought the time was ripe for a showdown with the Black community over carnival. They had also calculated that if they were to force a showdown they would win. In doing so, as subsequent events were to show, they grossly underestimated both the significance of the event to members of the Black community, and the capacity of that community to resist. At this time, the Black carnival movement was also showing serious signs of a split over a number of issues relating to the organisation and cultural development of the event. There was disagreement over ways in which to respond to the increasingly repressive state challenge to this important manifestation of popular Black culture. Aware of this, police strategists and hardliners must have been reinforced in their conviction that now was the time to force a showdown.

It was clear also that the police were aware of, and made the most of, the small but loud expressions of local opposition to the event. Having disregarded the overwhelming voice of the majority, and in particular that of the Black community whose event was at stake, the police and local authorities clearly listened hard to the voice of racist discontent.

Local opposition to the Notting Hill Carnival was focussed around a white community group called The Golborne 100, headed by George Clarke. It campaigned against carnival through its magazine *The Golborne*, mobilising opinion on the local council and in the police either to ban it, or move it away from Notting Hill. Several alternative sites were proposed, some of which were supported by councillors of the Royal Borough of Kensington and Chelsea. Included among them were White City Stadium, Hyde Park, and Chelsea Football Ground. On the relevant day, White City Stadium was occupied with greyhound racing.

George Clarke was a skilful campaigner. He played it soft and hard. On a subtle level, he argued that carnival, as a contribution of the people of Notting Hill to British life, had 'outgrown' the local area and needed to be re-located somewhere more suitable, preferably 'in the heart of London'. More stridently, *The Golborne*

BENEFIT IN AID
of
CARNIVAL DEFENDANTS

Acklam Hall Acklam Road W10.
Friday 15th October 8pm to 2am
with
SPARTACUS   SUKUYA
(leading london steel band)
and
CLASH

lights · sound system · fully licenced bar · food ·
donation boxes · admittance £1.
buses: 52, 7, 15, 28, 31. underground · ladbroke grove ·
westbourne park

BLACK DEFENCE COMMITTEE
notting hill branch

highlighted what the group's members saw as the inconvenience of the celebration, claiming them to be aberrations to the 'British way of life'. It pointed, in particular, to the effect of noise on older white residents of the area.

It is true that sound systems do not go for low decibel levels, and that 'unless you like the music, you're pretty likely to feel affected in some way'. But the Golborne campaign clearly identified the music of carnival as improper: they made no suggestion that elderly black people might be affected by the noise. The real issue was one of cultural accommodation:

> 'Many of us put up with fire crackers and other loud explosions on bonfire night, an English event. We have never complained. It is for whites to reciprocate with the same generosity when we have our celebrations. (Darcus Howe, the Road Made To Walk on Carnival Day: Race Today Pub. 1977.

All in all, the Golborne campaign diverted attention from the important logistical issues. In 1975 the Local Authority had failed to anticipate the numbers of revellers (building towards the estimated one million reached by 1986). No extra provision had been made for food or sanitation, nor had attempts been made to accommodate increased revellers and bands. Existing problems were compounded. In a downward slid which proved an effective countdown to the riots of 1976, the debate took on an ironic aspect of comedy as the Golborne campaign went on the offensive. In a radio interview, one white resident pertinently asked: 'You've already got one in Trinidad what do you want another one for?'.

State attempts at controlling the Notting Hill Carnival and containing its social and political impact reached their climax in the period between 1975 and 1977. Although this in itself is a brief slice of history, its significance is considerable because it echoes both the cultural repression of Caribbean colonial history, and the history of repression of popular culture and events of mass jollification in England.

Before the industrial revolution of the late eighteenth and nineteenth centuries, working people in Britain celebrated several open festivals and recreations which mirrored their life experiences, their hopes and joys, as well as extending their social milieu and breaking the routine boredom of daily existence. Such festivity, with its exhilarating human warmth and friendship, is well portrayed in 'The Collier's Wedding', by the eighteenth century poet Edward Chicken or in the nineteenth century writer Thomas Hardy's 'Under the Greenwood Tree'.

Several of these events were organised around such public occasions as Christmas, the annual parish feast and Whitsun, described by one oberser as 'a universal festival in the humble ranks of life throughout the kingdom'. Of the Christmas ritual in Northumberland in 1769 John Walis wrote:

'Young men march from village to village, and from house to house, with music before them, dressed in an antic attire, and before the . . ., entrance of every house entertain the family with . . ., the antic dance . . . with swords or spears in their hands, erect, and shining. This they call, the sword-dance. For their pains they are presented with a small gratuity in money, more or less, according to every house-holder's ability. Their gratitude is expressed by firing a gun. (R. Malcolmson Popular Recreations in English Society, Cambridge, 1979.)

Mass jollifications are well illustrated in English painting, especially by artists interested in depicting the lives of the lower ranks of society. Examples can be found in the work of William Hogarth, whose 'A View from Cheapside' depicts a revelling group of Londoners in 1761, including a Black horn-player. Thomas Rowlandson, similarly, offers us a glimpse of a hectic English fair in 'Brooke Green Fair. In the English life of the time there were numerous popular sports and pastimes, including football, wrestling, cudgels, ninepins, lying at alehouses and throwing at cocks. They sometimes attracted large crowds of working men and women. Inevitably such festive occasions also provided a platform for social and political satire, such as the 'mock mayor ceremonies' observed during the Easter holidays. In Randwick, Gloucestershire, for example, a mock mayor was elected each year from what one commentator uncharitably referred to as 'the meanest of people'. R. Malcolmson, op it

With the onset of the industrial revolution these popular cultural events were systematically suppressed by the state through a series of labour laws which imposed a rigid work schedule on the workers. Open air activities were curtailed. But the process of stopping fairs started even before this period: in 1761-2 alone, two standing orders from the Court of Quarter Sessions prohibited twenty-four fairs. More standing orders were subsequently published, until the number of fairs had declined significantly by the end of the century.

Open air events were particularly affected by land enclosure acts. Once the open fields used for such events had been removed by laws which imposed absolute rights of private property on land, it was often difficult to find alternative playing places:

'By the middle of the nineteenth century, any kind of open space for recreation was very much at a premium. The custom of playing games on public thoroughfares was no longer tolerated; enclosure usually eliminated any public use of agricultural land; and the rapid growth of cities involved the appropriation of much open space, some of which had served as customary playgrounds, for commercial building.' (R. Malcolmson op cit)

While the process of enclosure was welcomed by private landlords, one Berkshire landlord appeared to be more concerned and conscientious than others:

'I think some place should be provided for the exercise and recreation of the working-classes, and especially for their children. I have set out four acres at Oldsworth as a playground for the children, or whoever likes to play.' (R. Malcolmson, op cit)

Much of the official hostility to popular culture and working class jollification was underlined by a concern for effective labour discipline. As industry came to be seen as the lynch-pin of English progress, frugality, prudence and 'slogging' became the ideological images appropriate to its effective establishment. To the gentlemen riding on the tide of the industrial miracle, and transforming the world in its wake, traditional recreations came to be seen as self-indulgent diversions, wasteful of time, money and energy. One such gentleman, Richard Baxter, advised that 'all sports are unlawful which take up any part of the time, which we should spend in greater works'.

The historian Christopher Hill suggests that this emphasis on labour discipline derived particularly from the puritanism which held sway before the Restoration. In the morally charged debates of the time, the new industrial ethic came to flirt, quite curiously, with religious dogma that equated enjoyment with immortal behaviour and sin. Popular festivals came to be increasingly regarded by officialdom as occasions legitimising more degeneration and debauchery. The views of Josiah Tucker, though strong, were not unrepresentative:

'The lower class of people are at this day so far degenerated from what they were in former times, as to become a matter of astonishment and a proverb of reproach... we shall find them all agreed... to be the most abandoned and licentious wretches on earth. Such brutality, and insolence, such debauchery, and extravagance, such idleness, irreligion, cursing and swearing and contempt of all rule and authority, human and divine, do not reign so triumphantly among the poor in any other country, as in ours.

Attacks on popular culture were greatly helped by fanatical evangelical movements, among them the so-called primitive Methodists, who demonstrated at popular celebrations to 'undermine the influence of profane festivity'. By the end of the first industrial revolution, most popular festivities had disappeared or become 'domesticated'.

For the present, the Notting Hill Carnival and other offshoots across the country stand as significant symbols, crucial antitheses to this history of state repression. Their survival and development are therefore not the concern of the Black community alone, but of all who appreciate and cherish the vitality of popular creativity. The Notting Hill Carnival is now Europe's biggest street festival, and is unique in its display and expression of almost all art forms.

RESOURCES

Literature

1. Black Intellectuals Come to Power; The Rise of Creole Nationlism in Trinidad & Tobago by Ivar Oxaal. Pub. Schenkman Publishing Company, Inc. Cambridge Massachusets (1968). Library of Congress Catalogue Number: 67-29328.

2. **Words Unchained: Language & Revolution in Grenada** by Chris Searle. Pub. Zed Books Ltd., 57 Caledonian Road, London N1 9BU. ISBN 0-86232-246-4 (Hb.) ISBN 0-86232-247-2 (Pbk.)

3. **Masquerading: The Art of the Nottinghill Carnival** pub by the Arts Council Of Great Britain in association with Minority Arts Advisory Service. ISBN 0 7287 0514 1. An exhibition has been developed around this document inco-orporating photographs, installations, sound, video and other audio-visual media. For details concerning components and participants contact: Minority Arts Advisory Service, 25-31 Tavistock Plane, London WC1H 9SF.
   OR The Publications Office, Arts Council of Great Britain, 105 Piccadilly, London W1V 0AU.
   Caribbean Quarterly, Carnival Issue, May/June 1956 — Pub. University of the West Indies Mona, Jamaica.

4. **De Road is de Stage, De Stage is de Road** — First chapter of The Struggle for Black Arts in Britain, Kwesi Owusu (Comedia 1986).

5. **Carnival, the State and The Black Masses in the United Kingdom**. Cecil Gutzmore, Black Liberator 1.

6. **The Road Made to Walk on Carnival Day**. A Race Today Publication. Edited by Darcus Howe.

7. **Sparrow the Legend. Calypso King of the World. A pictorial history** — Available from New Beacon Books.

8. **Carnival. The Story of Carnival in Britain**. Edited by Michael La Rose. (New Beacon Books).

9. **History of the Voice**. Edward Braithwaite (New Beacon Books). Not a book on Carnival but discusses the significance of Caribbean languages and their relationship with popular culture.

10. **Caribbean and African Languages** — Morgan Dalphinis (Karia Press).

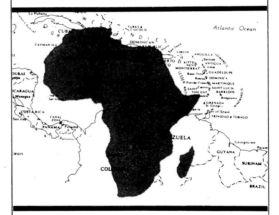

Caribbean & African Languages
Social History, Language, Literature and Education.

by Morgan Dalphinis

Karia ⓐ Press

11. **Carnival**, Wilson Harris (Faber and Faber 1985).

12. **African Music. A People's Art**. Francis Bebey (Lawrence Hill 1975).

13. **African designs, from traditional sources**. G. Williams (Dover Publications, NY 1971).

14. **The Mighty Sparrow**, CLR James. Essay in The Future of the present. Selected writings. (Allison and Busby 1980).

15. **The Trinidad Carnival: Mandate for a National Theatre** by Errol Hill, University of Texas Press, 1972. A near

definitive study of the Trinidad Carnival. New edition due out soon.

NOTE: The Commonwealth Institute, Kensington High Street, W8 (Tel. 603 4535) makes available a range of books, audio-visual information and teaching packs dealing with Carnival. Phone for details. Ask for information, Library Services.

Some Black Photographers (Carnival)

Ian Watts
David A. Bailey
Jacob Ross
Lance Watson
Ahmet Francis
Carl Gabriel
Sumil Gupta
Brenda Agard
Newton Brown
Ahmed Sheikh

background and context for the emergence of Carnival.

TERRITORIES. Directed by Isaac Julian, Sankofa Films.

MASH IN GUYANA

Rudy Grant

Film/Video

COCOYEA: A 20 min. 'short' focusing on the preparation and processes involved in getting a band on the streets. Visually strong, threaded with interviews and participants' commentaries. Available from CEDDO Film Video Workshop. Price: £30.00. Also available for hire. Tel. 802 9034 or 995 6994.

STEELBAND Metronome is another 20 min. capsule filmed by CEDDO examining pre-Carnival and Carnival activities centred around the METRONOME steel-band.

A TASTE OF CARNIVAL is a film produced by BLACK VISION, 649 High Road, Tottenham, N17. Tel. 801 8896. A 50 minutes long production that 'speaks for itself'. Produced, 1986 and covering Carnival Sunday & Monday. Sale price: £15.00. On hire only to club members.

FROM YOU WERE BLACK, YOU WERE OUT — Part of The Struggles for Black Community Series. Directed by Colin Prescod. Institute of Race Relations. On Black settlement in Notting Hill. Good historical

Carnival Arts Committee

Past Chairs: Fran Bynce, Selwyn Baptiste, Darcus Howe, Herbert Buhari, Louis Chase, Vijay Ranlal, Wilf Walker, Ossie Gibbs and Alex Pascall.

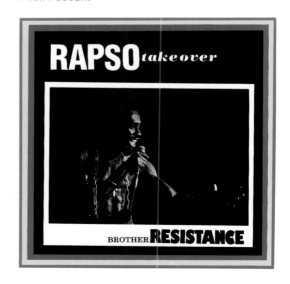

RAPSO *takeover*

BROTHER **RESISTANCE**

arrow

DOUBLE 'A' SIDE HIT

SOCA RUMBA

BILLS, BILLS, BILLS

TWELVE INCH SOCA 45

Some Carnival Highlights

Calypso Monarch — Competition for best calypsonian — held in the supertent adjacent to the West London Stadium.

Panorama Competition for best Steel Band. In supertent.

Carnival Gala — competition for Queen, King or Carnival — In supertent.

Brassorama — competition for best Brass Band.

Children's competition includes the choosing of Best Junior Carnival Queen, King, Male and Female individuals. Supertent.

Ol' Mas Dance — dance to welcome visitors. Then of course, Carnival Sunday — children mas on the road and the choosing of the best Costume Band.

Carnival Monday — a million revellers on the streets of Notting Hill and On the Road competitions.

Steel Bands — c/o Carnival Arts Committee

7 Thorpe Close, London W10 5XL.
Tel. 01-960 5266.
London Brotherhood of Steel
(Association of London based steel bands, c/o Tabernacle, Powis Square, London W11.
Ebony Steel
Glissando Steel
Maestro Steel
Mangrove Steel
Metronome Steel
Paddington Youth Steel
Star Dust
London All Stars
Juicy Steel
Lambeth Youth
Mo Dernners
Cockspur Steel
For Calypso and Soca records check Jet Star, 78 Craven Park Road, London NW10. 01-961 4422 and Orbitone Records.

CARNIVAL TIME

INNER FORCE

SOCA 45

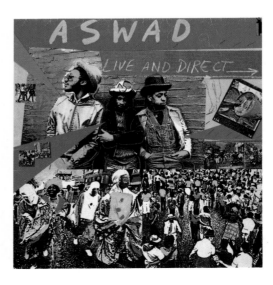

ASWAD

LIVE AND DIRECT

Brass Bands — c/o Carnival Arts Committee

7 Thorpe Close, London W10 5XL.
Tel. 01-960 5266
Inner Force
Kalabash
Carib Homers Odyssey
San Carlos Socarama Orchestra
Bachaks
Islanders
Marabuntas
Masquerade
Zagada
Cresondos Combo
Los Tropicanos
Rhythmn Makers Combo
Ivan Chin Combo

I. WATTS

90558 7408 /P 13 SEP. 1995